THE DRAGON-WISDOM CARDS

OF

ANCIENT CHINA

commentaries on The Tao
A guide to inner truth

MARK KUMARA

Order this book online at www.trafford.com
or email orders@trafford.com

Most Trafford titles are also available at major online book retailers.

Note for Librarians: A cataloguing record for this book is available from Library
and Archives Canada at www.collectionscanada.ca/amicus/index-e.html

Printed in Victoria, BC, Canada.

ISBN: 978-1-4269-0653-4 (Soft)

*We at Trafford believe that it is the responsibility of us all, as both individuals
and corporations, to make choices that are environmentally and socially sound.
You, in turn, are supporting this responsible conduct each time you purchase a
Trafford book, or make use of our publishing services. To find out how you are
helping, please visit www.trafford.com/responsiblepublishing.html*

*Our mission is to efficiently provide the world's finest, most comprehensive
book publishing service, enabling every author to experience success.
To find out how to publish your book, your way, and have it available
worldwide, visit us online at www.trafford.com*

Trafford rev. 8/26/2009

 www.trafford.com

North America & international
toll-free: 1 888 232 4444 (USA & Canada)
phone: 250 383 6864 ♦ fax: 812 355 4082 ♦ email: info@trafford.com

Joy is the outer expression of peace
Peace is the inner origin of joy
Love is everything in between.

(Mark Kumara)

ACKNOWLEDGEMENT

Visiting Taiwan in 1995, a student whom I had only met briefly and whose name I didn't know, gave me a packet of 55 photographs as I was stepping on to the bus to return to the airport. He told me he had drawn them from ancient texts and said they were a gift for me - "to do with whatever I liked". After some years of pondering what to do with them as they sat on my desk, I decided to make them into a wisdom pack. Meditating upon each one in turn, I wrote the 55 commentaries, which became *The Dragon-Wisdom Cards of Ancient China*. I have tried, through the Taiwan National University, and other different avenues, to attempt to contact this unknown student, but to no avail. I would like to thank him and unreservedly acknowledge his beautiful illustrations.

MARK KUMARA.
Denmark, Western Australia.
2009.

CONTENTS

INTRODUCTION TO THE DRAGON-WISDOM CARDS OF ANCIENT CHINA

The Dragon-Wisdom Cards of Ancient China consist of a deck of fifty-five cards which depict a story surrounding the ancient gods and goddesses, and demons and dragons of ancient China, together with a book of commentaries.

Each card has its own commentary which interprets the symbols illustrated in the card. The cards depict some of the mythological figures from China's rich and ancient past. Chinese people using these cards will gain a fascinating insight into their old religions. They may observe that - behind religion and ideology - there is a place where East can meet West in a spirit of truth and understanding. Westerners using these cards will find to their amazement that the ancient Chinese wisdom - which gave rise to such treasures as the *Tao Te Ching* - embodies all the eternal verities. These ancient gods and goddesses, with their dragons and their demons, talk to us from a past age. Then, their hidden messages were for a privileged few. Now, these ancient ones are ready to reveal their secrets to anyone who has eyes to see and ears to hear.

This hidden teaching, for so long concealed and disguised under the cloak of mythical images and symbols, is now revealed to be the framework of a great psychological and spiritual teaching. *The Dragon-Wisdom Cards* are none other than the tools for self-transformation and self-realisation. Readers will understand that I have interpreted these cards from my own personal viewpoint. My commentaries do not follow any traditional Chinese story regarding the cards and I ask to be forgiven if they diverge from any well known or familiar stories which the cards depict.

The fifty-five cards can be likened to a pictorial book. Each card depicts a psychological and spiritual profile of fifty-five different states of "being". Each of us, as human beings, in a past, present, or future lifetime, either, has faced - or will face - at one time or another, the psycho-spiritual challenges demanded by each of these states of being. There can be no escaping them. They are part and parcel of the human experience on the physical plane. When, with an open heart, with developed intuition, and immense courage, we harness our will to openly confront each of these states of being as they present themselves to us, we are sure to move through a transformation process. All that has been unconscious in us is ultimately made conscious. Integration of personality and spirit is realised.

At the very least it is clear that the symbols and pictures on the cards can be used as a guide to a deeper understanding of ourselves. The cards are instruments which effect the release of psychological blocks, and are helpful tools for growth. Especially, they can lead us to look beyond our personality concerns to a wider perspective and a deeper potential.

DIVINATION.

Tarot cards have a history of being used for fortune telling. Yet it should be understood that this is a superficial way of using divination cards. It needs to be remembered that a person's future can be predicted as a result of perceiving the unconscious patterns in a person's psyche. Indeed, unless we go through some inner transformation (making radical life-changes) the same unconscious patterns remain in us, enabling a reasonably accurate prediction to be made as to our future. However, the future of a self-realised person cannot be predicted for there is no unconscious pattern remaining upon which to base any prediction. The self-realised person lives fully in the present - in the moment. There is no past upon which to base a future.

Fortune telling, by using the unconscious for divination, affirms the unconscious - indeed, it perpetuates it. This is not a worthy use for these cards. The true wisdom of these *Dragon-Wisdom Cards Of Ancient China* is to be found in the providing of tools to confront and clear from the unconscious all that lies there *so that there is no longer any thought or feeling that is not conscious.* When all is conscious, all is light. The truth of the fact that "love is all" is then realised as being a most profound truth.

NOTE

When you are using these cards to give a reading for another person remember that in your essential nature you are a being of love and joy - and, that sitting opposite you is a being whose essence is equal in every way to your own.

From your own heart tune in directly to the other person's inner self. Look always to the inner life beneath the form. Use the cards to open your intuition to spirit's wisdom during the course of your reading.

Remember, so-called "negative" cards such as *Death, Greed, Lust, Anger*, and so on, are merely opportunities for transformation. Do not dwell on the mundane, or literal, meaning of these illusory and ever transitory states of being. These "dark" cards, indeed, are the greatest of teachers. There is illumination lying just behind them. Behind the fear and guilt that these cards might engender, there *is* love and there *is* joy. Look behind the illusion to the real in yourself and the other person. *Joy is the most real reality in this universe.* It has ever been so. Enjoy the "dark cards": they are a part of the Oneness. They have their role to play. But do not indulge in them or give them energy. Basically, they are there to show you not what you are, *but what you are not!*

HOW TO USE THE DRAGON-WISDOM CARDS OF ANCIENT CHINA.

1. Shuffle the cards well.
2. Choose the spread (see below)of the question you wish to ask. Then, holding the cards in both hands and placing them to your heart offer a short prayer to The Oneness. Ask for a blessing on your divination and ask that "the highest truth be made known to you".
3. Lay the cards face down, one by one on the ground or on a table, according to the design of the spread (below) you have chosen.
4. Now, turn the first card face up, contemplate upon it, then each card in turn and gently allow your imagination and intuition to speak to you about what the cards might be telling you regarding the question you have asked.
5. Turn to the required page in this book of commentaries of *THE DRAGON-WISDOM CARDS OF ANCIENT CHINA* for a closer examination and a reading of the commentary for your card.

NOTE

When first examining a card, allow your first impressions and your own intuition talk to you about the card. Allow your intuition to absorb all aspects of the card you have chosen. Listen to what it is telling you. This is your inner voice - your silent spiritual Self - communicating with you.

Then read the commentary. Use the commentary associated with the card to assist you in understanding it. If the commentary of the card you have chosen conflicts with your own interpretation of the card, ignore the commentary. This will strengthen your trust in your Self. The commentaries are best approached as a guide - and merely as a guide - to help you trust in your own wisdom and to throw light on your situation. They are not intended to take the place of your own wisdom which must, of course, always be your truest guide. Indeed, if the commentary for a card that you have picked does not ring true to you, waste no further time upon it. At least you will have learned where not to look!

If another question arises - or if you wish for clarification of your first question - pick another card. You may continue to do this until you feel your question is answered. Avoid the temptation of continually picking another card until you get a good one!

The commentaries can also be read, at any time, as an inspirational and insightful work in themselves. Of course, you may also use the cards using any other tarot format that you may already be familiar with.

SOME QUESTIONS YOU CAN ASK BY USING THE FOLLOWING SPREADS.

1. THE TAO SPREAD

This is a four card spread that you may use when asking about your spiritual path - in other words your own personal *Tao*. You can read more about the *Tao* in the commentary which goes with Card 1.

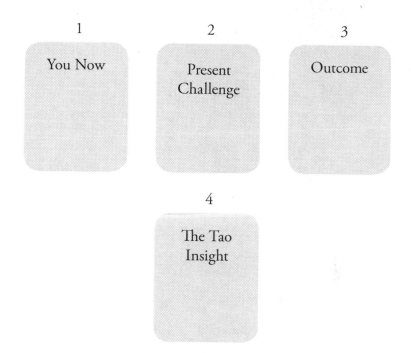

The 4th card is the *Tao* insight card for this particular spread. The *Tao* insight card can be likened to an overall view of your question - or, perhaps, the viewpoint of your spiritual or inner self which is at one with the *Tao*.

In this spread:

1. Card number *one* represents where you are now in terms of your psychological profile and spiritual achievement.
2. Card number *two* represents the challenge before you in terms of where you might be blocked. It indicates the direction in which growth is to be achieved.
3. Card number *three* indicates the outcome of this path after you have successfully met and resolved the challenge.
4. Card number *four* is the illuminating, overview, factor for this spread of cards.

2. <u>RELATIONSHIP SPREAD</u>

This four card spread can be used when you wish to ask a question about relationships. Use it in the same manner as THE TAO spread.

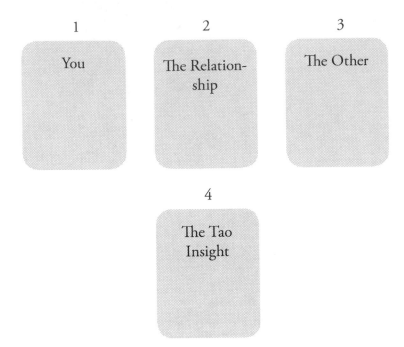

1. The *first* card is for you.
2. The *second* card is for the other person.
3. The *third* card relates to the relationship itself.
4. As usual the TAO insight card (the *fourth* card) is the overview of the relationship, observing it from spirit's viewpoint.

Use the commentaries to assist you in interpreting the answer to your question.

3. <u>WHAT TO DO? SPREAD</u>

This five card spread can be used when you have a question to ask about your purpose in life or when a decision has to be made about a course of action needing to be taken. In this spread the *fourth* card is the outcome. The *fifth* card is the overview card of spirit(the *Tao*).

1. Card number *one* represents the issue at stake here for you. It also relates to your purpose.
2. Card number *two* is what you need to be more receptive to, or more open to, in order to understand your purpose - or the issue at

stake. This card has to do with insight. It relates to your intuitive or feminine side.

3. Card number *three* indicates what positive action is required - perhaps as indicated in the commentary - for the issue to be resolved, for your intent to be refreshed, for your will to be re-harnessed and your purpose regained. This card relates to your male, or decision-making, side. It is your action card.

4. Card number *four* relates to the outcome.

5. Card number *five* is the overview card from the perspective of spirit.

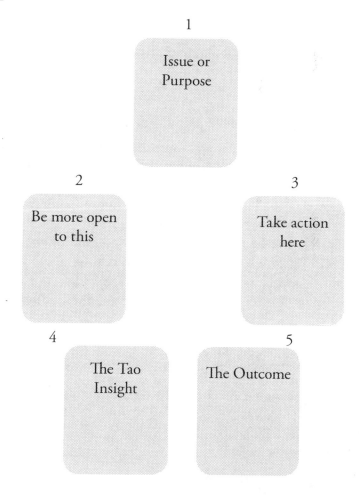

Remember you may have had many lifetimes, returning again and again to the physical plane. Only *one* of your many opportunities (in this lifetime) is being featured in this spread which is being highlighted for you today. Remember, that the past gives rise to a predictable future only as long as you remain influenced by your unconscious which drives you to repeat compulsions, and desires in an apparently endless circle (*the wheel of karma*).

When you are in realisation of, and enlightened to, the One Self, your past and future are now seen as aspects of the eternal NOW. This eternal NOW now becomes (as it always has been though you have been unaware of it) your eternal present. In this state of harmony, you are NOW at one with the TAO. YOU are the TAO at the centre of the circle. You are home.

4. MEDITATION FOR THE DAY OR WEEK

You may choose a single card at anytime or each day, and use it as your meditation card for the day. For a weekly meditation, choose a card at the beginning of each week, using it as your meditation card for the week. If the same card appears twice, you can take that as a sign you need extra meditating on that card! If you choose a different card to meditate on each week the fifty-five cards will open you to a wealth of treasure for exactly a year and three weeks. Use the commentaries to stimulate your imagination and develop further insight.

Remember, imagination is the key to developing both your intent and your intuition, being the royal gateway to fully-conscious awareness.

MARK KUMARA

1. THE TAO   (The Way)

A young man in a light sienna robe, wearing blue trousers is leaping through space. He has blue ribbons in his hair. The sleeves of his arms and boots are white. His hands are open. In the centre of his chest is portrayed the ancient Chinese yin/yang symbol of the Tao.

This handsome youth has a feeling of the eternal about him. He is carrying nothing. His hands are open. He is leaping through the air, unsupported by anything. Yet, he is looking down. His manner seems very composed, absorbed even. And, we might ask: is this what Lao Tzu, first Taoist Master and founder of Chinese Taoism, means, when he speaks of "absorption into the Tao"?

Lao Tzu left government service when an old man and travelled to the Gobi desert. There he left to the world a few pages - a mere 5,000 characters - of his teachings. This small book, the **Tao Te Ching** is one of the world's greatest treasures. Little known in the West, it is said to enshrine the wisdom of the universe. What is the Tao?

Tao means *The Way*. It is not so much a movement along a path, not even an attempt to create a way, but a profound transformation from limitation to liberation, through discovering and *realising* the way. The Tao does not exist sometime else or somewhere else, but is everywhere and at all times NOW. To Taoists, the Tao is the way that an individual has to be (or to follow) to be in harmony with the cosmic principles that govern his (or her) life instead of putting up futile resistance to them at the cost of needless stress and frustration. The teachings of the **Tao Te Ching** seem, at first sight, to be paradoxical or irrational, and to encourage passivity. But Tao, though meaning the way, doesn't point to any particular way. There is no fixed track to be followed. Tao has reality but no form. Little can be taught of the Tao. Lao Tzu says: "That which can be taught or put into words is not the eternal Tao." The Tao is not *for* anything or *against* anything, but it warns against

1

complexity, sophistication and cleverness as being corrupters of mind and spirit. The Tao, the Way of Great Life, overflows into everything that is in harmony with it. It is therefore the uncomplicated essence of what is right in your life: a way of *yielding* to a superior cosmic principle. It is easy, because the way *there* is best found by not making *there* your goal. It is the pathless path. *Ambition, longings,* the desire to make your mark in the world, are real hindrances. Actions tied to results or achievement are limitations. The Tao has no shape, but, like water, has dissolved within it all possibilities. In the words of Lao Tzu: "*One may designate NOTHINGNESS as the origin of the universe and BEING-NESS as the mother of all myriad things*".

He advises*: appreciate unflavoured things. As soon as the world regards something as beautiful, ugliness simultaneously becomes apparent. The Tao can be experienced without leaving home. The further you travel the less you will know. Silence is better than speech. Beware the distraction of the senses. Cultivate the having of less in your life rather than more. Power and learning is adding to oneself more and more; but the Tao simplifies you day by day. Submission is better than resistance. To be rigid is death. To yield is life.*

The Tao reveals that the One is the root of all things and, as a principle, penetrates and pervades all existence. The colour grey - a mix of black and white - in the symbol on this young man's chest, shows us he has achieved absorption into the Tao. He is no longer walking along the way. He is The Way.

Become The Way. Your way.

2. THE HEADLESS MAN RIDING THE TIGER   (No Direction)

A headless man in a brown robe is riding a red tiger. His head is sitting on his left lap, his eyes looking in the same direction as the tiger. His right hand is shown making a sign. His left hand remains hidden.

In Chinese symbolism the tiger represents the life force within. This card reminds us that unfocused or undirected life force, without vision, will lead to inertia in our life. Inertia will pull us inevitably toward the rocky path of form and animal instincts such as security, aggression, and sexual desires which are unloving - this being the lure of materialism unenlightened by spiritual awareness.

That this man has some spiritual awareness is evident by the sign (mudra) he is making with his right hand which is positioned over his heart. It is describing *chi*, being a name for life force or energy. This person is at home (see the brown robe) upon the earth. He enjoys being physical. He is aware of his power (the tiger) and is aware of his potential for great things in the future. However, he is sitting on his energy rather than allowing it to flow through him in a natural, joyful, and positive creative manner. This state of affairs may have arisen from childhood conditioning, from fears carried over from past lives, or from well meaning attempts to set aside the mind for a while whilst attempting to end the denial of feelings which have been long repressed. However, whilst it might be therapeutic at times to set aside the mind in order to explore feelings, it is not a good idea to make this into a life-style lest it become a chronic habit which seduces you into a life lived in limbo (the lower astral), leading to all sorts of disharmony which you will later regret as time wasted.

This card suggests a person who has put aside his head to allow himself to be motivated by his feelings, allowing himself to be carried along mindlessly. Yet, how can you be whole if you deny the mind? For, is not mind a legitimate part of the whole? The trick is, of course, to put your mind along side the mind of your higher self (being your enlightened mind) at the same time as honouring feelings, embracing the body and, most importantly, being truly open to your spirit (your expansive joyful energy). The person in this card cannot use their energy creatively for they have lost their vision. This amiable looking tiger needs direction from his rider. Together they can be a strong and formidable force in the world for good. Also indicated, is the possibility that you dismiss logic and avoid standing up for your beliefs for fear of hurting others, or, that, maybe you have the idea that being masterful, being in control of your own life - in other words, doing what you really want to do - will attract disapproval. You feel it is safer to agree with others, even if, secretly, you disagree. You may take a cowardly neutral position to avoid creating waves at all costs. Sadly, you are taking a comfortable, but spiritually stagnant, mindless, ride on an amiable over-fed stodgy looking tiger. Feeling your self to be a victim may also play a part here. Sitting on your energy, in denial of feelings - especially feelings of anger at your situation - you will experience frustration, boredom, resentment and dis-empowerment in your life.

The challenge here is to arise out of old habits. Impose some timely discipline upon yourself, recreate your vision, harness your energy, and take charge of your life and vitality.

3. THE MAN ON THE BUFFALO
(Resignation)

A sad old man in an orange robe, holding a stem of grass, is sitting on a green buffalo with yellow horns and a bright red nose.

This is rather a beautiful card at the same time as being, perhaps, deeply disturbing. There is a measure of peace here. A long and determined effort has brought tranquillity to the lower nature. The personality is stable and harmonious. It is represented here by the green buffalo. This is great work. Yet, it has been at cost - at the cost of joy and laughter, joy being the very heart of the life of a truly free spirit. For, what has been lost sight of here, (note, this gentleman's mournful, heartfelt, gaze downward toward the ground), is spirit - that inner, youthful, eternal essence of our being, that expansive enthusiastic energy that illuminates us with joy and makes us feel ALIVE!

This person has spent so long on the great struggle to transform the personality that he(or she) has forgotten that there is more to life than the struggle of self-discipline. If you create a belief system where there is always another problem ahead, or more pain to go through, or more fears to confront, your mind will construct unlimited, and ever more subtle, scenarios for you to deal with in order to satisfy your ego's belief that you cannot be self-realised until you have battled with the next problem. The compulsion to do this is like the compulsion to continue bashing your head against a wall only because you like the feeling when you stop!

His orange robe signifies his love of people. He recognises his social responsibilities and has the ability to listen with compassion to the sorrows of others. His buffalo, with its bright yellow horns, with its yellowish tinge to its sturdy body, indicates, however, that resentment at his lot in life and residual (unacknowledged) jealousy of the happiness of others still exists here. And, beware, anyone who tries to let him know of this; for, though he listens well enough to the woes of others, his own feelings he prefers to bury deep inside himself, not thanking anyone for pointing them out. His horns are formidable when aroused!

Fortunately, all is far from lost. Indeed, from the personality point of view, life is often a sad and a serious business - but from the view of your cosmic enlightened self (your holistic self) it is a mistake to take it too seriously. The green sprig clutched, protectively, in his hands, over his heart and chest, shows the way. All that this beautiful old man has to do, is, uncover and open his heart, and breathe in deeply the rejuvenating air of spirit. It will bring a smile to his face. That he has the will to do this is clear. The red nose on the buffalo indicates a strongly developed intuition which, when he trusts it, shows his powerful link to spirit. When he does trust it, he (or she) will find, to his (or her) amazement and delight, it will be all gain and no loss. Truly, all is joy. All else is an illusion.

Embrace, with trust and joy, your eternal spirit. And live life with a lightness of heart as an inspiration to all.

4. THE GIRL AND THE PEACOCK (Beauty).

A pretty young girl in a red dress is sitting on a blue peacock. The peacock's twin tail feathers are draped to the left. Both girl and bird are looking toward the right.

This card is all about beauty, and, irrespective of whether we are experiencing the world through the body of a man or a woman, the message is the same: beauty which is derived from integration and wholeness endures. Beauty that is partial does not. We are all striving, from life-time to life-time, for enduring beauty. Beauty, however, derived solely from the form is relative and ephemeral. It depends on the fickle and ever-changing perceptions of the dual relationship between the one who perceives and the one who is perceived (note the peacock's divided tail). So, we are talking here about the illusion of vision (beautiful though it may be) as against our own inner truth - the eternal reality of spirit.

First, the red robe that this beautiful young lady is wearing shows that she has a strong creative will. The handsome blue peacock upon which she is sitting indicates that she is able to express that will as spiritual vision. But does she?

Now, using creative will for meeting your desires: such as having a beautiful home, crafting a wondrous masterpiece of art, literature or music, or beautifying your body - or even the throwing of your energy into the healing arts, be it for people or the environment - are all absolutely fine, indeed, praiseworthy endeavours as far as they go. Yet, the use of will for inner change should not be lost sight of as this is where the will-to-good comes into its own as your own personal creative force for self-transformation. And, without self-transformation all that you have created in the outer world might, one day, seem to be rather irrelevant. Emphasising personality desires may lead you to contract your energy in the manner of a beautiful woman who finds herself in the position of needing to protect herself, thus closing down her heart (note how this lady is slightly hunched over her heart), due to the desires of those who would possess her.

It is as well to remember that the desire "to create your own reality" should be tempered by the understanding that your truth, your eternal reality, cannot be created to be any more beautiful than it already is. You cannot create what has already been created. All you need to do is to get out of your own way and allow the TRUE YOU (your higher self) to surface.

Rather than the creating of your own reality, the request here is that you surrender to the beautiful reality that you already are. All else shall follow. The fact that you are creating beauty around you, at the same time as doing the great work of self-transformation, is merely economy of energy. They go together. Priority, however, must necessarily be given, especially in times of change and crisis, to the requirements of your inner life.

Both the girl and peacock are looking in the same direction, toward the right. This is significant. This lady has vision. She has the ability to inspire and lead others by example. The challenge here is - whilst being a visionary - not to lose sight of your own inner work - that which is required to bring about your own enlightened destiny here on earth. This requires a certain on-going humility.

Look always to the life beneath the form and serve its needs.

5. THE DEMON. (Desire).

An obnoxious green demon with red ears and orange bands on his arms is holding a twin pronged fork in his left hand. He is squatting on the ground, looking up, and snarling angrily.

Here is a very explicit card about desire. Desire, if not attended to, becomes all consuming. All of us wrestle with desire in our lives. This is a part of the human condition and a factor in our progress toward fulfilment. Fortunately, not many of us allow desire to become so chronic, to become such a malignant force in our lives, that it completely blots out our link to spirit, debasing mind and feelings to the extent shown in this card. Vigilance is the watchword here. This card is a warning that certain desires - and beliefs associated with them - which we are hanging on to, are no longer useful. And it is no use us looking to heaven and railing at the injustice of it all. Closer to home, it hurts those we love when we take out our rage and frustration on others by using our nasty looking pitch fork.

Nothing in the universe can be done without desire. Desire is a natural, healthy, part of human existence and needs to be seen as such. However - and this is a big however - when that which is desired has outlived its usefulness it must be let go of, else you become a slave to it (note the slave-like bangles on this demon's arms). The Buddha said: desire is the cause of all suffering. Rather, it is not desire itself that is so much the problem as the attachment to the results of the desire in question. Letting go, learning how to be still, allows your inner spirit (your higher self) to be in communication with you once again. It also allows others the space and freedom to follow their own path, thus benefiting everyone. This is good work. It will take you to where you wish to go: the fulfilment of your Self upon the physical plane - integration of mind and spirit (without being dominated by astral influences). This is self-realisation.

Refusal to listen (note the red ears) to the prompting of your spirit, to let-go of whatever it is you are now being asked to let go of, must lead, inevitably, to a powerful negative state which will take a powerful hold over your personality for which no one is responsible but you (see how the demon is sitting in his own puddle!). This may give rise to rage at the unfairness of life, rage at the universe (or at God), feelings of powerlessness, blind fury, or a determination to get your own back and stay "hating". We may have feelings of being betrayed, feelings of self-destruction, or of self-loathing, despair or suicide (note how he is clawing at himself with his right hand). This demon is determined that his position is the true one. He is refusing listen to anyone.

In this universe of duality there are two basic opposing desires (or forces). The first, attractive to un-awakened humanity, is toward expression in form. Attachment here can be said to be the *satanic* influence at work. The second, which is attractive to spiritual seekers, is toward the desire for union with the Oneness so as to be the Oneness. Attachment to this idea can be said to be the *luciferic* influence at work. Both ignore the Higher Self which stands between the two as The Christ Principle, here in the eternal NOW, in joy and love.

This person is risking devolution and spiritual suffocation. He or she is being entombed by his or her own concrete belief systems at the expense of openness and vulnerability. If remedial action is not taken to confront this situation with firm, compassionate, and detached self-analysis, this person is heading for a serious disease. The unpleasant result of energy sent downwards, tied to the demands of the instinctual form life, results in anti-social behaviour, giving rise, alas, to a vengeful and demented mind.

Stop! Be still! Stop trying to make your life work. Regain your connection with spirit by remembering who you are. Live and let live. Acceptance (another word for love) and letting-go are necessary.

6. A MAN WITH A GOURD.
(Poisonous Thoughts).

A man wearing a grey skull cap with a ferocious expression on his face is pointing with his right hand whilst his left hand grasps a magic gourd or calabash. From the mouth of the gourd curls a strange spiral of smoke harbouring a ghostly pair of red eyes.

Just because we don't actually see our thoughts in operation in the air around us doesn't mean that they are not scurrying around, working, for good or ill. They are. So, this card is about the power of thoughts - especially those with the power to wound.

It is said that an enlightened person - a master - does not think of another person without automatically seeing that person as an enlightened being. Of course, the master will notice the person's problems, but without any condemnation or imposition being made upon the person. If the person who is observed is already seen to be whole then that person is, essentially, lacking nothing, and therefore nothing - no thought, good or bad - will cling to him or her. Until we reach this state of grace, however, we do need to watch our thoughts and be aware of the damage that they can do to the well being and self-confidence of those we think about - even if only in passing.

Thoughts are the creative stuff of the universe. They are especially helpful for creating an environment, a planet, a country or a home in which lessons can be learned and the particular requirements of our spirit (our higher self) met. Unfortunately, they also have the power to destroy, to minimise, to suppress or repress, or to distort reality to such an extent that the essence of our spiritual truth becomes veiled, clouded, and confused, to the detriment of our *being* and of our link with spirit. The resulting denial of feelings gives rise to suffering.

11

This card reminds us of our very real responsibility to become aware of our thoughts - yes, even the casual stray ones - and to closely monitor and guard any tendency to judge, condemn, criticise, otherwise put down, dominate, or control others to our way of thinking (which includes prurient sexual desire). The deliberate direction of mental energy toward another is an imposition. When done with malice and intent it is surely evil. The gentleman in this card is being less than gentle in thought. With his *right* hand, he *right*-eously makes accusations. In his left hand he holds a nasty looking stew-pot of poisonous thought. This man is determined to be right, and to seek revenge. Perhaps he is a political zealot or religious bigot. Perhaps he feels let down or betrayed. Thoughtless gossip is harmful enough, but this man is not merely a gossip. He is going to put down those he thinks oppose him at all costs and fight for *his* rights, condemning all who stand in his way - especially those who have the temerity to disagree with him, or those who he feels have slighted him. Reflect, however, upon this: this sender is still left holding his gourd with its evil genie inside. His thoughts are still connected to *him*. Whatever you send out will one day return to *you*. You will be left holding the baby - in this case, the evil! So, beware! You must defuse your evil thoughts before they contaminate you irreparably. How about trying some old fashioned forgiving, or allowing - or letting go?

The admonition here is to guard your thoughts.

7. THE ANGRY BLUE MAN.
(Frustration).

A man with a blue face and blue hands wearing a blue garment and a blue official looking hat has been placed on a blue card. Flames are coming out of his head. His mouth and beard are bright red. His hands are loosely tied by a scarf. His right hand is open like a claw.

Here is a very angry man. Here is a dragon king overcome by passion. Wrath is here personified. So, then, why all the blue? Why the sky blue of spiritual vision which is closely associated with justice, liberal thinking, equality and freedom?

Yes, this is all very well, but freedom denied, leads to frustration - with explosions of anger (red hot air!) always a possibility. Indeed, in the case of feelings being chronically suppressed over a long period of time, it will be necessary (and heartily therapeutic) to release the energy that lies within the emotion of anger by expressing the anger. This should only be attempted in a supportive therapeutic environment lest you cause damage to yourself or others. This important emotional "work" is essential. It will expose old belief systems which are suffocating your spirit. It will allow you to make new choices in your life that will affirm your true being rather than bolster an ego that has been conditioned by the opinions of others.

This card signifies - as frustration always does: conflict. The fury this man is feeling is being denied its fullest expression because he feels that his hands are tied. In other words, he is aware that he is in a position of responsibility (note his official looking hat); he is aware that anger is, in most cases, hurtful and counter- productive; but all the same he cannot help himself being angry. His fury is as much directed at himself as at the object of his rage. In his heart he knows this and, of course, this makes him all the more angry.

There is in fact no such thing as justifiable anger, for anger has little to do with justice - indeed, it usually escalates any affair into one of confrontation and enmity. Anger, does, though have a lot to do with fear. Your own fear. In the case of a person with moral integrity and responsibilities, the usual fear is the fear of things not turning out right. So control is a big issue here, It is the "I know what's right for others" syndrome.

However well meaning you are in your caring for others, it is as well to remember they have their own life to live. To allow those you love to make mistakes can be the hardest thing. Everyone has the right to their own self-expression. So, to allow others, once committed to their purpose, to be foolish without interference is in itself a loving act. Patience is here required. Indeed, who is there to judge the merits of one fool from another? When we are wise we see that there is no one.

Mental confusion surrounding these issues leads this person to feel trapped and remain trapped in a situation which, though socially acceptable, does not nourish his or her inner life. We have here an intelligent person of integrity and position caught in the trap of divided loyalties - though, if you were to look deeper, you would find denied feelings.

The challenge before you is to take a step back from your present responsibilities and re-assess if they are really deeply nourishing for you. If they aren't, either let go of them completely or do them in a different way.

8. THE PANTHER MAN.
(Independence).

A blue man is wearing a pink and red coat, and green trousers. He is sitting on a leopard, holding an axe behind his back.

One of the most striking aspects of this card is the similarity of expression on the face of panther and rider. It is the kind of warning expression that a cat makes when all it wishes to do is to be left alone. This animal is not in an aggressive mode. On the contrary, it looks relaxed. It is, however, very alert (note the waving tail!). It is, moreover, quite at home with its rider. They seem happy with each other as if they are a good team.

Here we see magnificent independence - with the ability to live uncompromisingly to the tune of your own spirit. Anger (the axe) is behind you now, well integrated into your being, to be used only occasionally in exceptional cases - and only as a clearing energy at the dictate of your spirit. There is harmony in the lower nature (note the green trousers) and your pink coat indicates an affectionate nature and an open heart. Your amazingly blue face and hands indicate a playful and youthful (remember Krishna) nature combined with spiritual vision. Your energy, your body and ego are in harmony with one another. In other words, you are close to enlightenment - maybe you are a bodhisattva, or a world helper, or a teacher, with your own important work (first) to do in the world.

For those of you who pick this card and feel that you are not (yet) in the league of world servers, it is as well to reflect on the lessons that the cat has for us. For, although a cat has no intellectual awareness of its own possibilities, it nonetheless lives in a state of grace that can teach us much. A cat moves where it is comfortable, sleeps when it sleeps, loves when it loves, eats when it is hungry and purrs when it feels content. It moves swiftly away from discomfort and only fights when it really has to. A cat is far too intelligent to waste its time and energy proving to itself, or to others, that it should stay tied to some place where it is uncomfortable. Further, a cat is very naturally itself. It is the very essence of independence. It is quite at home with its own brand of felineness. Can you imagine a cat spending its time wondering how it might become more feline? No, it would become quite neurotic in this vain attempt to solve the unsolvable. And so, you might well ask yourself: how can I be more naturally myself? What feelings am I denying? Am I too introspective? Am I too self-analytical? Am I terrified of being alone? What am I seeking from these cards?

To be a natural human being is to enjoy the unique experience of being one. But to go deeper, to open your self to your own stillness and surrender to your own inner grace, is to discover your own inner light, whilst at the same time delighting even more in your human self.

Observe the hours that a cat does nothing but sit gazing. Insight meditation is to do with watching. It is to look without looking. It is watching without any mental connection to that which is watched. It is going deeply into your body and just being there. When all that is seen disappears, only the watcher remains. Then a tremendous moment arises. To know it is to be forever fearless, to be full of love, to be immortal.

Follow uncompromisingly and without hesitation the dictates of your spirit, and honour the perfection of your own divine design.

9. THE KING WITH THE FLYING FOX. (Protection).

A powerful man, left foot forward, right foot bent under him, is squatting on the ground. His fists are clenched. An aggressive looking flying fox is sitting in his arms.

We all know of someone who is the tower of strength, the very corner stone, of some organisation; who is the consummate administrator, the able doer of good works with the ability to hold it all together. This person is King (or Queen) of their sphere of influence. This card represents such a person. It is an insightful card. It is showing us that power and the use of power may attract an equal and opposite reaction which needs to be understood and somehow dealt with.

The use of power, coming from personality desire, will always have a boomerang effect. Whenever there is a *demand* by the user of power to see his or her schemes succeed - in other words, if he or she is attached to the results of this demand (or desire) - the user will experience hurt.

In Australia, "the tall poppy syndrome" is the name given to a quirk in social behaviour where high fliers are routinely subject to attack and vilification or *cut down to size*. However, let it be said: if the high flier (the tall poppy) has no attachment to results, no hurt will result. In this case, the attack devolves back upon the person who instigated it, leaving the user of power (the tall poppy) still feeling good about himself or herself. What we are saying here is that goodwill is the best protection. Then no other is needed. Right thought (harmless thought) and an open heart is natural protection. Putting up barriers around yourself, and the maintaining of them, for whatever purpose - emotional or psychic - takes energy: your energy. How often have you heard people say: "This person makes me feel tired. He must be taking my energy". It is not so. What is taking your energy is your own sense of powerlessness in the situation accompanied by the fact that you are draining yourself of energy by unconsciously erecting barriers for your own protection. Building barriers is tedious for the soul and wearisome for the body. It takes energy to build them and energy to maintain them.

By far the best protection is self-confidence, a trust in your own spirit, an open mind and an open heart. This card indicates a person of considerable strength and purpose but whose mind is closed to any ideas other than his own (note the closed fists). He is unbending. His feelings are heavily protected, and probably denied. He will see any attempt to get close to him as a possible threat. Anyone who does succeed in getting close will be in danger of being attacked - or severely put in their place. See how this King (or Queen) maintains his barriers to avoid confronting his fear of being seen to be vulnerable. There is a strong belief here that to attack is the best means of defence. And, yes, a dog is the most loyal of subjects. Yes, the fox is noted for its sagacity. Having loyal and wise companions around you can undoubtedly flatter the ego. But, with left foot forward and right foot bent, this King is not about to fly in the eternal NOW. The dog is protecting his heart, *but does it need to*! It could be said that this *dog* which, when reversing the letters, makes up the word *god* backwards, is blocking his heart. He will not let anyone in. Too much cunning and sagacity feeds the ego. It is to be too clever by half. But where is an open heart and wholeness? Sadly, all his good works can never make up for his deep insecurity, his low self-esteem and his lack of self-love. For him this is a tragedy. If this situation is not rectified, this capable entity will become an embittered lonely old man. So, the challenge here is to look at your life from a different perspective. You need to share your feelings more and not take life so seriously. You are not indispensable. And remember, you are greater by far than anything you will ever do.

Be aware of the vibration you carry around with you on a daily basis. Enjoy being wrong sometimes, admit to mistakes, and get in the habit of having a good belly laugh.

10. THE MAGICIAN.
(The Master of Illusion).

A child dressed in a loin cloth, his hands in a prayerful position, is standing upon two fiery wheels. He has six other arms attached to his upper body, mostly holding various implements.

Here is the Chinese god who came down from heaven to confront the Monkey King. He has many arms, suggesting many talents. He is also a being of simplicity (note his simple apparel). But, perhaps, most striking of all is his youthfulness, and the sense of peace and strength, emanating from his face. The general stance of his body is one of controlled purpose. His hands are closed over his heart in the universal sign of worship, in acknowledgment of inner divinity. We all know of people who seem to have the knack of being good at many things: all they turn their hands to turns to magic. This is such a person. This person is also aware and at peace with himself. A double achievement. Here is a master magician.

Discipline of mind is a prerequisite for enlightenment for it is only by stilling the mind, by observing the illusions it throws up, by honouring but being unmoved by feelings (the astral currents), and by experiencing what is beyond the mind (your spiritual essence) that the mind is put in perspective, *and the real is known.* Your mind is merely a tool which is yours to use. Mind is not your all. Feelings (the astral) are not your all. Joy is your all. Love is your all.

Wisdom arises (being an end to suffering and karma) when mind is the servant of your all - that truth which lies behind mind. This truth existed before mind ever was or ever will be. It is the eternal I AM - the very essence of yourself. When realised, you return to the outer world a changed person, and the mental discipline you have acquired along the way is now very useful to you for it is at your disposal to use in any way you wish. And, what could be better than to live in harmony with your spirit (your truth), to trust in the universal life (the Oneness), to live in the eternal NOW (attuned to your Higher Self, the Christ Principle) and use any of your multiple skills (garnered through many lives) which are appropriate to meet the need of the moment. You are now the owner of many skills and the master of them all - each now being illumined by spirit. You stand in truth, in detachment, in mastery of the material world - able, spontaneously, to change direction at a moment's notice (note the wheels under his feet). You have many gifts to give to the world. It is your joy, both to serve and give them. Yet, above all, remember all is moving towards harmony.

The negative aspect of this card for those who are not enamoured of the idea of self-mastery is that you might be attempting to be all things to all people. You hope for the best but experience confusion in your life from the many bewildering choices that seem to confront you. Much energy is wasted in trying to hold it all together. You dabble at many things but are master of none - and certainly feel unfulfilled. One hand knows not what the other does. You live in a whirlwind of different ideas and have not yet found your centre. Your mercurial skills take the place of the love you are desperately seeking in your heart. Your feet (your wheels) move in different directions. You are heading for the splits and an uncomfortable spill!

You were born on this earth already a master, this card is to remind you of this fact. You know who you are. Have confidence in your skills and trust your spirit. Your way shall be shown to you. You are here to externalise yourself upon the physical plane. Above all, trust in the NOW. Illuminate each moment with your joy, your peace, your compassion, and your strength. Exemplify harmony.

11. THE GUARDIAN. (Alertness).

A young man, heavily armoured, stands with feet apart, holding a spear in his left hand.

This young man appears to be on guard. His posture is erect, his stance stable and he has a purposeful demeanour on his face. He has the air of someone who knows what he is about and he is going to guard his integrity against all comers. This is fine as far as it goes; but does not guarding your interests - clothed in such extensive armour - not smack a little of fanaticism?

In psychological terms, armour is the protective mechanism we put around ourselves (often unconsciously placed in childhood) to avoid feeling; because, to feel requires us to remember how we were hurt - and are probably still hurting. We don't wish to remember being hurt, so we paint a marvellous camouflage over the surface of our life, where we even deny that any hurt ever happened. Here is a man wearing garments of many colours. Yes, he is determined to make a good show of himself, wearing brightly coloured clothes to dazzle, and perhaps to deflect the interest of those who might seek to look deeper or get closer. It has the feel of a uniform about it. Uniforms are much loved by those who lend their energy to mass movements, who look at unity as an outer goal rather than an inner one for each person to attain in their own way, in their own time, with their own spirit. Indeed, his spear and upright stance, right hand on hip, indicate a rigidity of mind and a determination not to be gainsaid.

It is well to remember here, that idealism - which at its worst becomes fanaticism - is counter-productive if: you are so attached to the outcome of your ideal that you become emotionally unstable any time that ideal is threatened. If you maintain you are not emotionally evolved, but at the same time need to protect yourself with armour, who are you fooling ? In this situation, peace is an impossibility. Love and joy are absent. Now you are mimicking strength. You are brittle and graceless, without flexibility. Rigid. Defensive. What you are left with is unbending self-righteousness. You will grow stiff and even more brittle with age until, hopefully, you snap one day in a strong breeze (when a compassionate enlightened mind - a master mind - mirrors to you your own ego driven mind) and you experience a timely *letting-go,* or, alternatively, you will keep building up armour until it suffocates you, and you can't breathe. So what to do?

What is required here, apart from a sense of proportion and a liberal sense of humour concerning your pet vision and your identity attachment to your all-important vision, is mainly three things: 1. An inquiring DEVOTION to your inner life. 2. HUMILITY (the ability to listen). 3. ALERTNESS.

Alertness of mind is essential if you are to become aware of how feelings are being denied. When you are in denial of feelings, mental clarity (stillness) is impossible to achieve. Without mental alertness nothing is possible. This soldier prince is showing great alertness for the outside. It shouldn't be too difficult for him to alter his mental focus to be alert to the inside - to his thoughts and feelings.

And, now, let it be said: your vision, *in this very moment,* is right for you. Your religion is right for you. Your spiritual path is right for you. Your opinions, and your concepts, are right for you. They are not necessarily right for anyone else. There is no need to convert others to your way of thinking. What a relief!

But - and let this be a big BUT - be open to change. Live in the NOW. Be more spontaneous. And ask yourself: where, NOW, are my opinions and concepts? Where, NOW, is my vision?

Who are you protecting yourself from, and why is it necessary? Who is the YOU that needs protecting?

12. LOOKING BACK.   (Indecision).

A man wearing green armour, clutching a spear in both hands, is looking backwards whilst running forwards.

A spear is an item that you throw forward, yet this man is looking backwards. Here there is a longing to go forward but a reluctance to let go of the past. He is hanging on to his spear, so tightly, it has more the appearance of a security blanket rather than a weapon for the future (the spear being a symbol of adventure, based on truth, thrown confidently into the future). But, perhaps, we can understand. Is it not one of our greatest fears: the stepping off into the new, the unknown?

To avoid acknowledging this fear - being nothing less than our attachment to the past - is it not one of our most cunning psychological ploys to grasp at anything new; anything which gives us the illusion of moving, or growing, or being useful? The truth is, of course, that by grasping our new vision over tightly it has no room to breathe. There is no room for spirit to bring in those wondrous imponderables and unexpected bonuses that give any worthwhile vision a magic life of its own. You can't throw your spear forward while you are holding on to it for your very life.

This man is in conflict. No vision of his can manifest to any degree of success unless this is resolved. Successful vision requires total commitment. If you want to be successful at business you must be total about it. If you want to be a useful politician you must be total. If you want to be a top athlete you have to be total about it. If you want to be enlightened your life must be a total commitment to enlightenment. Otherwise, you will fall between two stools.

You may go backwards or go forward, this way or that way, but once having made your choice, stick to it lest you fall in the middle. To be total is to be whole. Anything else leads to disastrous life-sapping indecision. Note: to be total doesn't mean you have to be stuck with something for all time, or, indeed, a minute longer than you wish to be. Being total means being total IN THE MOMENT. Then the next total moment leads to the next total moment. These total moments add up - on the physical plane at least - to a sequential line of beautiful total moments: your life. When you are total in each and every moment, moving with strength and purpose, with poise and self-confidence, your vision assumes a new perspective. It doesn't dominate your life. You do not NEED it to support a deprived personality. The means to an end is seen, NOW, to be as important as the end itself. In fact, the means becomes the end - and the end, the means. There is no separation. No difference. No duality.

Indecision leads to self-disgust and anger (note the amount of dark red in his garments). The colour of his dark green armour is in contrast to the clear apple green colour seen in the aura of healers. He is masquerading under a posed pretence of harmony which is deeply false. He needs to realise that his roots are not where he comes from in any physical sense. When your life is rooted in spirit, you are HERE. Looking back, exploring your physical roots, can be therapeutic but should never be seen as the final answer to your fulfilment. Truly, your roots are not to be found in your social background, but in The Oneness and in the Light. Hanging on to your concept of your future whilst looking back, is not going to attune you to your Higher Self.

Not being prepared to resolve or face fears from the past is a recipe for a fool's paradise: you are clinging to your outer symbols for security whilst running scared inside.

Harness your will and face your fears, totally. Open yourself to a new vision and commit yourself to it. Trust in your spirit at all times and live in the moment, totally. In all you do, be total.

13. THE LION KING.
(The Will to BE).

A black man in a red robe, with the visage of a lion, is holding two staves in his right hand. His left hand is stretched out in a commanding manner.

The first impression one has of this fascinating card is one of power. Surely his outstretched hand is saying: STOP! ENOUGH! COME NO CLOSER! Here is authority. Self-knowledge. Determination. Here is a strength which comes from the unassailable position of self-awareness. But there is also simplicity. Note his simple garb, sandals, no weapons, merely two staves, neither of which he is holding in a threatening way but cradling to himself as if they are the symbols of his office. And so, in a sense, they are, for this man is at home with power. He is an initiator and his staves represent the forces of duality now under the dominion of his spirit (his right hand). They are his rods of power. He does not consciously use power so much as to allow power to express itself through him to go where it is needed.

The colour black (being the absence of colour) is very significant. Black here does not mean dark, negative or evil. It indicates that his unconscious - the invisible or "dark side" - of his psyche has been fully integrated with his personality. No feelings are being denied. No illusions cloud his mind. His vision is of spirit (note his inward looking eyes). He looks to his inner life for his outer motivation. This man will not suffer fools gladly. He will see the games that people play and the entangled scenarios that suck them into suffering but he stands clear and allows these things to touch him not. Hence the command to stop! Stand clear! This is the path of the Zen master. His wish is to stand alone, being in the world but not of it. His desire is not so much to be a creative force in the world but to BE in the world. This WILL TO BE is from the heart. Its colours are ruby and gold (note his golden hair and the golden amulets on his arms). It is not the power *to do, to change or to heal*. It is the power of BEING. This is the power that is experienced when all is seen to be ONE, in the ONE, as the ONE, so that, essentially, there is nothing to do and no one to heal for all is already perceived as BEING WHOLE. The Lion King says: "Stand back. Come no closer unless you are ready to give up all and enter the reality of your own truth".

This card is for someone who is very close to self-realisation. The end of all doing is in sight. The cessation of all desire is all but upon them - even the desire for enlightenment. This is a time for simplicity, independence and aloneness, and being true to yourself. This is a person, man or woman, who, with leonine strength, but soft golden hair (the symbol of a radiant aura) is saying to the world: " STOP!

You hold no more interest for me and I ask you to let me alone to live my life the way I wish to. You will no longer take me away from myself. I am a free spirit". This is the point in your life when you need to say the big NO. It is a firm but compassionate NO to anyone who would bind you with their expectations of how you *should be* in order to accommodate *them*. It is time for you to beat your own drum and follow your own spirit. It is the big YES to *your* life. Maybe you will face the terror of your loneliness and arise as the Lion King, (as Osiris, the invisible Lord of the ancient Egyptians) - the power behind the throne of all creativity, the WILL TO BE.

Live your truth. Let your NO be your NO and your YES be your YES. Follow your spirit uncompromisingly.

14. THE LADY WITH THE MANDOLIN.   (Growth).

An attractive young girl, wearing fine clothes, is carrying a large bundle of grass on her back to which is tied a pipa (a Chinese stringed instrument). Her hands and feet are hidden.

Why is such a beautiful young girl, dressed in such fine clothes, carrying a bundle of grass on her back? Is it burdening her down? Hardly. Yet, how can she play her Chinese mandolin, smothered as it is by all that grass? Perhaps this is the reason she doesn't look very happy. There is a doleful (or is it dutiful ?) expression on her face and her general demeanour is one of compliance rather than happiness.

This is a card about growth, youth and creativity. These are intertwined in our lives and create for us much confusion. After all, if we were to arrive on earth as fully realised entities there would be no need to go through all the phases of physical growth, and the many years of mental and emotional struggle. We would have no need of mothers or fathers, teachers, or therapists - or of society's benevolence. We would have come here uncluttered by any and all of this. We would be already living our truth. We would be free to experience this earth, its magic, its wonder, its diversity, and the unique experience of being on a physical planet of such natural abundance, without any anxieties whatever. We would be without the compulsion to interfere, to improve on, or to meddle with this masterpiece. Every moment would be one of curiosity and wonder. Every moment would be an affirmation of joy and happiness, and celebration. So, why isn't it?

Simply put, it is because our need to grow physical bodies and adapt these bodies to physical living has caused us to forget who we are. It is: because for years people have been telling us what they think is best for us. It is: because for years - indeed, lifetimes on end - we have been doing *our duty* by our family, our tribe, our clan, our nation, our religion, our guru, but NEVER doing our duty by our self. Unendingly, we have been indoctrinated by the ideas of others, that others have put into our heads, starting on our mother's knee, continuing on into school and university. Especially insidious are the religious teachings that teach us absurd stories of hell and eternal damnation, of guilt, suffering and sorrow if we do not follow the prescribed teachings laid down by the religion we find ourselves belonging to - luring us into their clutches with tales of paradise if we do. Particularly obnoxious are religions that believe they are better than others, deny equal rights to women, and go on so-called holy wars. This is not religion. This is control. This is politics in disguise. Nothing could be more ugly, or more calculated to confuse or distort the truth.

This person is still moving to another's tune. Her (or his) past is behind her but she still carries it along with her. Her hands are not her own to use. Her feet tread not her own path. All is yet hidden. But all is far from lost. Note the stars on the beautiful blue gown this lady is wearing. She needs to drop her bundle, take hold of her mandolin (her Chinese *pipa*) and sing her own song. She is going to be a star. It will put a smile on her face.

It is time to let go of all that is behind you, gently but firmly. Have confidence in your future. Sing yourself into your own truth. Bring your joy to the world. It needs you.

15. THE SEER.   (Skill).

A woman in a gold gown, bent at the knees, is blessing the world with her right hand. Over her left shoulder are seen nine, violet, bright eyed birds, all looking in the same direction. She has a quiet smile on her face.

After all is said and done; all the philosophy, all the religion, all the politics - and all the great works that are done; the masterpieces, the music, poetry, art, healing, together with all the heartache, disappointment, and sacrifice, which go to make up our short stay in this world, what is it that endures? What remains after all this effort? What do we take with us when we leave? And, intriguingly, what can we bring back with us should we wish to return to this world in another life?

The answer is *skill*. What we have done is long forgotten. Can you remember all the details of your first bicycle ride or the first few books you read? Maybe not, but still you can read and ride a bike. And, in a world which is so beset by fears and anxieties, what greater service could there possibly be than to use the ancient and time-honoured skills of a seer and a wise woman for helping people confront their fears. This is a woman who does just this. This is a woman who is a mid-wife; not a mid-wife for the bringing of physical babies into the world, but a mid-wife of consciousness. With her skill she eases, encourages, provokes, the bringing forth, from deep within fearful unhappy personalities what has long been hidden: the light of radiant consciousness. To be born again. No greater gift can someone give to another than to assist another to find their own inner light: the realised Self. This gift endures. It is eternal. It is a gift greater by far than the sacrificing of your physical life for another.

This card represents the skills available to you that you can access: knowledge, wisdom, insight and intuition (the nine violet bright-eyed birds). They come from your feminine (left) side. The colour violet indicates that the energy is for transformation, for yourself and for others. As we assist others, so we assist ourselves. It goes together. It is economy of energy! The number nine is significant. It is the number of abundance, of bountiful gifts. Also, nine birds plus one woman make *ten* - the symbol of wholeness. This woman has integrated her personality with her multi-dimensional Self. In other words, she is attuned to her Higher Self. She blesses the world with her right hand and is ready to serve those who will approach her for the many gifts she has to offer. She is not pushing herself forward. She is content that those who come are meant to find her. Yet, in her quiet way, she is flying. See the invisible chair she appears to be sitting upon. She might almost be sitting on the proverbial broomstick! She is quietly and confidently supported by her inner life and knows exactly what she is about. This lady has wings and reminds us of the ancient Egyptian goddess, Isis, the benefactor of Egypt, who brought learning to the peoples of that land. Her golden robe, with its light green spirals and trimmings, suggests balanced creative power. Around her neck is a collar of clear ruby indicating uplifted creative energy at the throat centre, for the sounding forth of the WORD. Her personality is centred in the dark blue of deep space.

Open to your spirit and your inner voice. You are here to give of your gifts and use your skill in the world. Trust your insights and bless the world with your grace.

16. THE BLACK KNIGHT.   (Control).

A black, heavily armoured, knight with a red beard, carrying an axe in his left hand, sits astride a lion-dragon which is roaring out its defiance at the world.

This card is all about deceit and control, at the back of which - as always - is fear. Here is a powerful entity who has gained many skills but in this life has chosen the path of control instead of that of self-knowledge. He keeps his fears hidden - out of sight, out of mind - under his armour. His very presence (see that glare in his eyes) is enough to put the fear of God into anyone who might even question him. His axe (left hand) will quickly demolish anyone who is bold enough to disagree with him. His right hand is stroking his beard, deceitfully pretending wisdom. But, alas, it is a false, confusing, wisdom. He speaks with authority, but it is the authority of unresolved anger which seeks to dominate rather than to uplift and clarify. His voice is red with passion, but not loving passion.

This person - whether it be man or woman - is suffering from a deep hurt in their psyche. Their unconscious (the black power) is being heavily protected by personality armouring.

Whilst this state of affairs continues the soft inner promptings of spirit cannot be heard (note the thick helmet over his head). He must use deceit and hypocrisy in his daily affairs to pretend that all is well. He uses his powerful, well-developed, personality to control a situation to his satisfaction. His bottom line is almost certainly *security*. Loss of security leads to vulnerability, and this he must guard against at all cost lest he be forced to acknowledge the ancient wound within.

Of course, this state of affair cannot be expected to last for ever. The resources of the personality are finite. The energy required to keep up this pretence inside this wall of armour, unable to be replenished by spirit, will become an unbearable load on the personality. Eventually the personality life of this man will disintegrate. If his inner wound is not dealt with in this life-time it must wait for another. But it is far better to deal with this inner monster (the lion-dragon) sooner rather than later, lest you project it outward to those near and dear to you, giving rise, later, to regret and guilt. Of course, it only seems to be a monster. But, needless to say, unless you deal with it, it will ride you for ever.

There is no doubt who is the dominant force here. The personality rules. The rider, cowering in his armour, assumes a strength he knows perfectly well, on the inside, he doesn't possess. Huge feelings are being denied here. In esoteric terms, this being might be called a dark master. His whole life-force is channelled into controlling his own feelings and, of course, the feelings, and hence the freedom, of others. Plenty of people may be seduced into following such a dark lord. But, they in turn, will also be in denial of their spirit and their feelings. Perhaps they are looking for an outer saviour - so as to avoid acknowledging their inner pain, or their inner life. All is not lost, however. The monster can be acknowledged with love. It can be recognised and confronted. It needs to be, for you and it are hurting. You will be amazed by the peace and joy that integration brings. All is gain. That which can be lost needs to be. So, see to it.

Seek help with humility and become a true master. It will be the most courageous thing you ever do.

17. THE MADMAN. (Madness).

A blue man with three heads and six arms is prancing about in a frenzy. His eyes, including a third eye, are staring wildly. His clothes are a collection of motley items. Dark red flames are playing about his head. His feet are sprouting claws. One hand is ringing a bell, others are carrying a seal and daggers.

The history of human religious activity suggests that as such activities go, both orthodox and unorthodox, it inclines the human personality towards eccentric behaviour which often seems to border on madness. The term "madness", however, has long been discarded by psychologists. What is madness to one culture might be quite acceptable to another. For example the shaman of Asia and Siberia is said to receive messages from the dead and commune with spirits. Yet, his mental balance is so insecure he can easily lose self-control, attacking anyone who provokes him. His eyes bulge and stare out wildly, his face undergoes hideous contortions, and on occasion he will roll about on the ground screaming and foaming at the mouth until he loses consciousness. When he regains it, he is himself again. From earliest times "the falling sickness" was regarded as divine in origin and those who suffered it or induced it by drugs were possessed of a special link with the gods. If you believe this, you'll believe anything!

That some people should see this odd behaviour as divine shows how out of touch with their own warm, loving feelings some people must be. The fact is, this is just one more ploy by a deeply fearful ego to refuse to acknowledge and face its inner terrors. Instead, it projects them on to the outside with all manner of psychic fantasies and emotional frenzies, hoping, that by so doing, attention will be firmly and for ever focused (note the attention-seeking bell) on himself. Of course, amongst superstitious people, carrying on in this manner guarantees status in the community, giving its practitioner a dubious mystical power over its gullible members (note the intimidating swords).

Mental displacement - the deliberate (or unconscious) closing of the door on your spirit - usually results in either deep depression or frenzy, both being desperate attempts to deny deep feelings of an ancient hurt, guilt or rage. This card represents a man who has some spiritual knowledge (note the open third eye) but, alas, the fires of his lower three vehicles - mind, emotions and physical body - are dominating his life. This is indicated by his three heads surrounded by dark red flames. His animal nature is in complete control of his life (note how he treads the earth with clawed feet). Instincts and emotions reign. This is insanity. His personality is using insanity as a protective mechanism to avoid awareness of deep feelings which might otherwise be brought out into the light of day. He is suffering from wounds long denied. Yes, a self-realised person may appear unconventional at times but in no way will such a person rant and rave with wild staring eyes. Wholeness brings about integration of mind, body and spirit. It brings a profound peace into the system. The focus of attention (and one's energy) is away from the outer towards the inner. Every cell in the body is alive to a new message of love and joy. Illusion ends. Peace and clarity, and harmony - the purpose of life here on earth - reign. You become divinely ordinary.

Stop all doing. Sit. Look within. You are in danger of becoming addicted to energy. You are not going towards energy, but towards peace. "Be still and know that I am God".

18. THE BATMAN.   (Jealousy).

An elf-like creature, part man, part bat, with clawed feet and bright blue hair, is holding a hammer in his right hand. He is striking at a dagger he is holding in his left hand. His lower garments are a dark cloudy green. His upper body is armoured. He is the Chinese god of thunder.

This card represents a person, who has some spiritual vision (note the blue hair), who has gained some measure of control over the lower nature (the green lower garments), but whose heart is armoured, and whose thoughts and emotions are directed towards a dream solution to his problems. He is fixated in his desire, but thwarted.

Jealousy is like a dagger in your heart. When projected on to another it can give rise to feelings of murder and revenge - or a wish to obliterate another person from your own personal universe. It doesn't let you sleep. It doesn't let you rest. It brings no peace. It is thunder in the soul. It comes like a thief (like a bat) in the night. Like a vampire it drains away your energy. It gnaws away at your vitality. In your waking life you are a mess - at best you only just manage to keep your life together. A person embroiled in jealousy is caught in a web of their own making, and the spider at the centre of the web is their own mind. No matter what the jealousy is about: be it about money, power, a lover, position, artistic gifts, popularity, it is a state of mental restlessness, behind which lies *resentment* at your predicament. Behind this resentment lies fear, and behind the fear is ignorance of your own true divine possibility in this physical body.

Jealousy is desire contaminated by fear. The fear of loss. It's a loud noise in your mind. Now, "desire" is the will of the Oneness manifested upon earth in all creatures. For humans, there is *correct desire which is nothing less than the will to be self-realised* (being your ultimate possibility in this lifetime); then there is incorrect desire (the illusory need to protect self) which is manufactured by your conditioned mind (your ego) to

Mark Kumara

support and protect itself by every devious means to justify its own actions, and to avoid facing ancient fears and feelings long denied.

Jealousy has the insidious habit of masquerading as correct desire - as in: "I want my rights", or "I want justice". But it isn't, and soon enough its brown suffocating wings will fold around you, comforting you with an illusion of hope, but closing off your heart. A brown cancer has found fertile ground on which to feed. At the back of incorrect desire is the fear of loss, of aloneness, of being without love or the ability to love, of being without a body or the means to experience, of being ineffective or of not achieving, of being trapped or helpless and, of course, fear of spiritual failure. These are deep fears. They are the daggers in our heart. All human beings carry them. They need to be acknowledged with love and compassion. In a sense, on this physical plane, they are natural enough. It is easy to see how they have arisen. *But they are an illusion. They have outlived their purpose - if indeed they ever had any.* Now is the time to face them, feel the terror, and, as you do, see them fade away like mist before the rising sun. They have had a hold over you long enough. Their time has come.

Insight is the means by which desires, and attachment to the objects of desire, dissolve back into the Oneness. Change your perspective. Live in the here and now. Learn to be spontaneous. Let go. Breathe in love, breathe out love!

19. THE MASTER IN THE HEART. (Wisdom).

The upper half of a wise old man is framed in a fiery heart. A small flame flickers from the top of his head. He is carrying, over his shoulder, a fly whisk in his left hand. His right hand is stroking his beard. He is the Chinese master Tai Shang, master of alchemy.

This is a most beautiful card in this pack of the *Dragon Wisdom Cards of Ancient China.* What can we say about it? This man has achieved. His white hair and the fiery heart are the ancient Chinese symbols of wisdom. Wisdom is the flower - the child - of love and knowledge. There is nothing more this world can teach him. His sole link to the world is his compassion for it. In the time remaining to him in the physical body he will assist those who are drawn to him (note the fly whisk over his left shoulder to whisk away stray or illusory thoughts). Now he has become a beacon - a bringer of life. He feels no obligation to the world (his burden is light), but he still feels love. Love is his achievement. He knows - because he can *feel* it - that he *is* love and he is embraced by love. His awareness, together with every cell in his body, is that ALL IS LOVE. Fear is over. Anxieties are at an end. Peace reigns. Joy and humour bubble under the surface of his mind. He is embraced by the heart of all life.

To the world, what has he to offer? First, himself as an example. Second, his wisdom (his right hand is stroking his beard). Third, his energy - his life. He is now an open conduit for the life-giving love energies of a realised universe. To be close to such a man is to gain a taste of what is waiting for yourself. It is not to be missed. Yet, neither is it to be clung to, for, remember, there is, in the end, no outside master. There is only the master within your own heart. You are a master unto yourself. This, then, is probably the message in this card. Meditation upon the master in the heart is maybe now necessary for you.

Once we have gained some control over our lower nature, once we have acknowledged ancient wounds and become aware of feelings long denied, no longer suppressing them - yet, at the same time having the mental discipline to make wise choices as to what emotion we choose to express, we are ready for the work of meditation and contemplation.

Meditation is a means to an end. It involves focus and concentration. It is still you *doing* something. Contemplation, on the other hand, unlike meditation, has no focus (*See Card 53. The Watcher*). It is just BEING there; you and all-that-is, just being together. Just watching. It is the end result. In both contemplation and meditation, awareness is everything. Meditation may be watching the breath, or thoughts. It may be focused on light somewhere in the body - or it may be the wonderful meditation of the master in the heart.

In the meditation of *The Master In The Heart*, sit comfortably (or lie down) and, using your most loving and skilful imagination, create, in the region of your heart, a picture of an (imaginary) master - as beautiful, as loving, as happy and wise, as glorious a figure as you can possibly conceive him or her to be. Strongly visualise and see this figure surrounded by a soft blue or gold light, whichever you prefer. Feel your love pouring towards this image. Concentrate upon it for a few minutes. Finally, look deeply into his (or her) eyes. Now, go behind the eyes. Move into union with this beautiful person who actually lives inside you. Feel the joy, the peace, the bliss of this union. Try to remain aware of this presence within you when you resume your daily activities. This is the master in your own heart. Indeed, it is your Self. To know this is to remember who you are. It is the great meditation. It leads to contemplation.

Seek the master in the heart...in your heart.

20. THE SOLDIER.   (Obedience).

A soldier, in heavy armour and black boots, stands with feet apart, sword in hand. His left hand is tightly clenched. He is clean shaven. Behind him is an auric diagram of colours. His expression is one of grim determination and undying obedience to his cause.

Your personality (your conditioned ego) is comforted by a sense of belonging. Whatever it is you belong to, whether it is to some group, to a religion, or to a nation, or even to an ethnic race bound by the colour of your skin, this bonding of yourself to a cause is undoubtedly enhanced by facing a common threat. Uniforms are invariably worn by those defending such enterprises. This card is about control, and control doesn't stop at clothes and weapons: there may be physical requirements such as hair style, tattoos, or circumcision. More serious, however, is the invariable requirement to relinquish individual thought, and to require the individual to deny his or her feelings in the service of the greater cause - that cause being, of course, one designated by someone who wears a more important uniform than you do. Obedience to the cause is everything. Obedience to the uniform, or the all-important creed, becomes an act of patriotism and heroism. The mind becomes empty (note the absence of any colour behind this soldier's head) of any desire for self-expression. Indeed, the colours surrounding him are a stylistic representation of his aura. Note how rigid, how defined, the colours are. Here is no soft blend, no gentle melting, of colours. Here there is only right and wrong, and no in-between. His left hand, tightly clenched, shows he is firmly closed to messages coming from his feminine (intuitive) side. This man has become a robot at the service of his masters. Whether these masters be generals, priests or politicians, it matters not. Press a button, give an order - and he will snap to attention. Give another and he will go out and kill. Point him in the right direction and he will die for you. He has given up his will.

Here we have the crux of the matter. We might ask: is it ever useful to be this obedient? Is it ever useful to surrender your will to another? Unequivocally, we can say no it is not. And no justification will ever make it so. For what purpose, then, is your will?

When your outer life is in harmony with your inner life, your highest potential is actualising on the physical plane. This is love in action. It is also the manifestation in the physical world of directed purpose - purpose directed by your inner life (being your Higher Self attuned to your spirit). Now, it may be useful, for a while, to give up your will *temporarily* to someone you trust who can show you the nature of your conditioned ego and the illusory games it plays.

Understand, always, that your will is, first and foremost, designed for the heroic task of unmasking your fears and illusions so that, one day, in one life-time, you can realise your SELF as a totality. Indeed, this is the great work for which your will is designed. Obedience to another's will, or to the dictates of society, family, church etc, need to be examined carefully to see whether they are in line with your own higher good toward this eventual grand purpose. Remember, there is nothing wrong in putting duty first if that is what you want to do. There is nothing wrong in being creative. If there is joy and enthusiasm present in your life, so well and good. If not, proceed cautiously.

You are conditioned by beliefs and attitudes that may not be in your long-term best interests. Be open to change. Honour your feelings. Enjoy groups but resist becoming entangled in them. You are unique.

21. THE PLAGUE.   (Evil)

A green man with three heads, each with a prominent third eye, is wearing an orange and red coat. He is crouched forward, pointing two swords at the ground. Other arms are holding up a flag which warns of the "plague". He is waving a bell, and shouting.

All through our life messages bombard us like the plague. Everyone seems to have something to say to us, and we to them. And, here, again, is someone else with yet another message.

How strange! A man with three heads! It shows us that his three personality vehicles, mind, emotions and body (his three green heads) are all involved. His open third eye shows that this person has some spiritual vision. But - and this is the big but - is his message really for you? And is it a vision of the heart? If not, run from this person like the plague. Evil, remember, may be a deliberate attempt by an unscrupulous entity to confuse, or to infect, to dis-inform, or to manipulate you for financial or emotional reasons. Evil may also result, in the long-term, from over zealous goodwill.

How to know if a message is for you? Be alert! Put it to the test of your intuition. Is it for your higher good? Is there a feeling of expansive joy there? Spiritual messages are not always comforting. More often, they are designed to confront, and generally prod and encourage you to change your way of thinking - indeed, to go beyond thought. It can bring up much fear. The age-old symbol for this is "the burning away" of the old. Fire! Hence the fiery red coat of this messenger. Old beliefs and attitudes, long entrenched in your mind, need to go. The flag you have been flying, living under, must change. This fiery awakener is ringing his bell to attract your attention. The two swords in both hands indicate the need for severing all ties to your old beliefs, both from the male and feminine aspects of yourself. The swords are not raised but pointed at the ground. This is to remind you that the intention of the messenger - and the message - is not to hurt you or leave you bereft of all support or nourishment. It indicates, merely, that this "work" must be done on the physical plane. This is not to say that the most important benefits for you will not be apparent until after you leave this plane for another.

When you are thrilled by a spiritual message, it is as well to *digest the message* and not be overly attracted to the messenger. A teacher that has your best interests at heart will say, "Look not at me, look where I am pointing". And it will be toward you that he will point. He will point at your fears and anxieties, and then he will demand (perhaps entice you, cajole you, and in every way induce you) that you confront them. He will keep pointing at these illusory aspects of your conditioned ego until all have melted away and you stand revealed in your naked, and immortal, glory. However, as the saying goes: there are helpers and helpers. It would be a sad world if no one helped anyone. But you need to understand there is a limit to the help even the greatest of teachers can offer. There must always come a time when YOU MUST MOVE ON, returning to your own self for your own answers to your own destiny. The outer world of glittering "masters", promising rosy futures, performing magic, casting their alluring spells around gullible disciples, you may leave to their own devices. They are truly like the plague, easy to catch, hard to escape from. They are not for you. Unless, of course, you wish to discover what you are not!

Never be afraid to speak out - when inspired by spirit.

22. RIDING THE LION.   (Strength).

A man, lightly armoured, carrying a ceremonial sword in his right hand, is sitting on a lion. He has a grey moustache. The lion has a blue nose and a blue flame is sprouting from the centre of its head. A cloud of grey breath is coming from its mouth.

This card has an unmistakable feeling of strength about it. The man is sitting very solidly on his lion. He looks at home. His lion is a magnificent creature, proud and strong, its four feet firmly on the ground, and, despite looking suitably fierce, there is an undoubted hint of playfulness about this lion. The lion's blue nose indicates a developed intuition linked to spiritual vision, as does the blue flame coming out of its third eye centre. This person is firmly attuned to spirit. Being attuned to spirit is often likened to being in the presence of a cool gentle wind (note how like a fan his sword is). The grey cloud coming out of the lion's mouth is particularly interesting. We know that grey in the aura indicates emotional repression: denial of the life force, but here it indicates a combination of black (yin) and white (yang). In this case grey represents the out-breathing of an expression of unity. The shape of it looks like a tree. What could be stronger, yet be more harmless or more whole than a tree?

True strength comes from the integration of spirit, mind and body. Fake strength (which is merely brittle *force*) is a ploy of the conditioned ego. Ego-based strength has behind it neither the direct intuitive awareness of spirit-linked consciousness nor the immovable strength that spirit-awareness brings. It is a shaky strength, being a protective device to maintain the ego to its best advantage in whatever role it is currently playing. It has no permanency. True strength is based upon an inner awareness of your life energy (spirit), an awareness of your creative role in the scheme of things (intuitive mind/higher self), an attuned practical mind (creative mind), an awareness of your feelings (emotional/astral body), and, lastly, a true honouring of your body of flesh (your bio-dynamic space suit!) which enables you be here on this physical planet.

It can be seen, therefore, that the key to true strength is *awareness*. Awareness leads to self-knowledge. This in turn leads to self-realisation and enlightenment. Many life-times of seeking brings about final integration. It is the goal. And, once reached, the goal fades away to become a new way of life: now the whole universe is as wondrously open to you as your home. This can only be achieved on the physical plane, for the physical plane is both the plane of limitation and the plane of demonstration. The physical plane is also very much a part of the whole - albeit a small part. If you cannot be whole here, you cannot be whole elsewhere, for always a part of you will remain in fear or in denial, or be unresolved. Wherever you go in this universe, the physical universe goes with you (in an energy sense, at least). It is a part of you. It is a part of the whole. And you are a part of the whole. It needs to be accepted and loved and integrated into the whole. Humans need to acknowledge *the pain* that forgetfulness of their origins (from spirit) has caused. The fear and guilt that has arisen during this time of forgetfulness is huge.

Awareness, insight, self-forgiveness and reintegration brings about true strength. It leads to a profound peace in your whole person out of which comes a natural expression of the joy of your being.

Realise where your true strength lies. Listen to your inner wisdom, and trust uncompromisingly in your spirit.

23. RIDING ON THE BULL.
(Power).

A warrior, in golden armour, spear at the ready, is riding a highly coloured bull. Both bull and rider are looking to their left.

There is nothing that personifies power more majestically in nature than that mighty male animal, the bull. In this card the male (*yang*) virtues of strength, courage, assertiveness, detachment, leadership and independence, are indicated. They are qualities every bit as important as the more fashionable feminine qualities of gentleness, intuition, wisdom and compassion.

This card represents a person who has achieved much spiritual progress. The mainly blue bull together with the warrior's blue robe indicates spirituality. The rainbow coloured bull further tells us that he has many skills and attributes to draw upon. This warrior's golden armour represents the golden aura of his presence. His basic energy (his power) has been transmuted upward into "gold". In other words, all that was dark (hidden or repressed) in his psyche has been lifted up into the light of day and integrated into his whole being. His heart is open as shown by the opening in his chest. The colour black is often used to depict power. When this man speaks, he speaks with words of power (note the black beard). This is a man who knows who he is and what he is about. He will not suffer fools gladly, and he will defend himself at all cost from anything which might threaten to seduce him into forgetting who he is. Note how his stance is at-the-ready, looking toward the left. This is more of a defensive action than an attacking one. This, then, brings us to the question of what is the right use of power.

"Power" is the energy you have at your disposal. It is known by the strength of your aura. It is your presence. When you actually use it, it becomes force. So, we can equate power with *being*. And force with *doing.* Now, *being* and *doing* are like yin and yang. They are like opposite sides of the same coin. In this physical world of duality - this world of active demonstration - there can never be just one or the other. In other words, *being* will always contain within it an element of *doing*, and *doing* must necessarily come out of *being.* And this is the relationship between power and force.

It is impossible to say what is the right use of force, for who is there to judge what is right or wrong? Every entity upon the earth is using his or her mind (the force) in their own way as, indeed, they are entitled to do. Right use of will, however, (the desire behind all forcefulness) is best applied in the direction of self-knowledge and self-realisation. For, then, force, when used, is used with good will in the service of wholeness. When integration has been achieved and wholeness realised, you are automatically in tune with the whole for the good of the whole. Your ego-mind, that part of you that has the curious ability to create for itself an exclusive little world of its own, *apparently* separated from universal mind, will have made the great surrender - the great fusion. Now you are no longer alone. You are home. You have regained your roots. Now, *you are the power, but also you are love.* Now, power is just there, so to speak, as a harmless - yes, harmless - but natural ingredient of love. And love is seen to be - not a romantic wishy-washy type of love - but truth manifested, a truth that may sometimes hurt (but never harm) in action. This is the power of love.

You need to become aware of the difference between power and force, and how you use force. Power is harmless, force may not be.

24.A MAN ON A CLAY HORSE.
(Depression).

A man wearing a green hat, holding two crossed swords, is sitting on a pink clay terracotta horse. The horse is leaning backwards on its haunches. The man is smiling.

We all know someone who is full of grand thoughts and great schemes, invariably involving themselves but whose wonderful ideas never seem to see the light of day. This card indicates such a situation. This wooden-looking, clay, plump pink horse is not going anywhere fast. In fact, despite its rider urging it to get going, it seems to be protesting bitterly, lethargically sliding back on its hocks. Yes, indeed, the crossed swords of the rider indicate there is a dilemma here that needs resolution before life can enter the situation and restore rider and horse to a natural and buoyant state of enthusiasm for life on the physical plane.

This man has achieved a measure of self-knowledge and harmony in his life (note his green hat and green beard). He has an affectionate regard for himself (his pink horse). This gives him a certain amount of self-satisfaction - even, at times, happiness (note the smile) and yet there is a large part of himself that is still in denial. He strongly believes he is moving. But anyone can see he is not moving. His head is full of nice dreams but on the earth all is blocked - or, at least, they seem to be blocked. There is a deep conflict here which needs to be examined. Whether he knows it or not, this is an indication of a depressed personality.

Depression, born out of the many anxieties that beset humans, is a common disease of the times. It is prevalent amongst those who live in our technical so-called "civilised" society. There are so many pressures: to achieve, to perform, to absorb knowledge, to support, to do the right thing and be the right sort of person, that we become like a rudderless

47

boat in a mill pond, losing our integrity, and deep down we hate every minute of it. On the surface we keep up a smiling face.

This can go on for only so long, until we slide - often unknowingly - into depression. Severe depression may lead to a "nervous breakdown". Such a breakdown is our cry for help. And help we definitely do need, because depression appears when we have exhausted our own resources. We no longer know which way to turn. So, we stay stuck, and either pretend to be enjoying it or make up some nice self-justifying story in which we pretend that this is really the plan for our life. Yet, deep down, we know we are fooling ourselves. If this is allowed to become a malignant way of life it leads to chronic low self-esteem which can be difficult to shift. At the root of all depression is the denial of our life-force. We dis-empower ourselves for the sake of our beliefs. Usually, these are beliefs about what we think we *should* be doing as against what our life-force (our spirit) *feels* we would like to be doing. The anti-dote to depression is to reclaim our power and only do what we really do feel like doing! Feelings long repressed and deeply buried must be brought up, expressed, released and life changes made. When you trust in your spirit (when your deepest desires and enthusiasm are linked to your energy) and, when you lovingly inform your body and mind that you are giving yourself permission to accept this new state of affairs, life will embrace you again. Spirit does love to move!

Let go of all outer considerations for a while whilst you explore your true desires. Honour them. They are the gateway to your future.

25. THE DARK KING.   (Lust).

A black King in shiny metal armour with amulets on his arms is standing, feet astride, right hand outstretched, grasping a spiky club in his left hand. A fiery ball of sexual energy is emanating from a cloud of black smoke. It joins up with a similar stream of smoke coming from his mouth.

The desire for union, like an electric current, runs through all of creation. It is a force, therefore, to be reckoned with. It is better to understand it and work with it than to pretend it doesn't exist or to live in denial of it. In humans it expresses itself as sex.

Humans, being individually conscious, are able to transform their consciousness whilst living within the physical form. Indeed, it is important that they do so, so that each can take his or her place in the universe as a fully integrated universal entity, having attained spiritual awareness (mastery) at all levels. This is achieved by the unifying of all the elements within a personality, with spirit; thus ending all unconscious residue. Now the higher self can shine through. This is self-realisation. This union whether we realise it or not, is the goal of all human endeavour. The desire for union is the means by which the individual is propelled forward, as it were, to realises this goal. Where love is present, sexual union between humans creates more love. It produces radiant energy, and provides insightful mirroring through which the individual can see aspects of themselves hitherto unrealised. This all helps in making conscious that which is still unconscious. A useful spin-off of physical sex is that it is the means by which physical bodies are provided to entities who wish to enter the physical plane.

The gentleman in this card, alas, has fallen into the trap of lust. Lust is that mindless desire for union with an outer form that runs through the life of form. His lower creative centre (sex) is on fire, generating black smoke. His higher creative centre (the throat) is resonating in sympathy with his lower energies. The two centres are joined in a pact of desire in which the lower is dominant. Instead of his higher creative centre being used to re-create himself into a transformed consciousness (sounding forth the "word" of unified creation) this man is allowing himself to be dominated by his instinctual desires. The *mindlessness* of lust is not at all the same thing as the ability of a sage to enter into the state of *no mind*. The blind urge of lust longs to grasp (note the open right hand) what is desired, emphasising duality. Mind may appear not to be there, but it is very much there, powerfully swamped by emotion. The sage, though, in his state of *no-mind*, observes his mind and allows his emotions to become still. He does not blot out thought, but explores the spaces between thoughts, to what is behind mind, to what existed prior to mind, to what is true and eternal. He seeks the source of all-that-is and unity. The nasty looking spiked club reminds us that the mind has many subtle and not so subtle ways of grasping what it desires, or justifying to itself what it "needs". It reminds us of the snakes on the head of the Greek goddess Medusa which, when looked at, turned you to stone. Irredeemable lust will eventually turn any heart to stone. Loveless sex, far from being nourishing, ages the body and psychically scars the personality.

This card requires that you examine how you use your sexual energy, in thought and deed. Motives need to be looked at. Openness with your lovers and friends is necessary. Old hurts and fears need to be acknowledged. See the divine in your partner. Live in the NOW instead of fantasies.

26. THE MAN OF VISION. (Vision).

A man in blue pantaloons and a dark green jacket is riding a fiery, red and blue, dragon, with green horns. He has two hands coming out of his eye sockets. The palms of these hands contain his eyes.

This man is looking at life through his hands. His vision of himself and his vision for his future is tied to what he believes he must achieve. He is closed (blind) to any realisation which doesn't envision success in terms of an outer goal. He needs to be doing something to be happy. "Doing" is more important to him than "being". His goals are all important. Results are what matters. Ends take priority over means (and we all know what a hard hearted philosophy that is). Indeed, without anything to do, this person will feel a failure. Fears will arise. He will suffer insecurities and low self-esteem. He will slide into depression. Why is this?

Essentially, his personality is not yet sufficiently integrated with his spirit for his "doing" to come naturally out of his "being". His conditioned ego-mind has formed a world of its own in which he lives, supported by many self-justifying attitudes and beliefs about his position in this cosy little scheme of his. In order to maintain this "dream" he must often deny feelings which might disrupt or shatter it. This alienates him from his body which is always a sure and perceptive receiver of spirit's wishes. Notice how rigid, how stiff-necked and erect he is. He and his dragon (his physical body) don't look comfortable together. There is no integration. He is merely sitting on it. In fact, they look as if they are about to head off in different directions. His dragon is a magnificent animal, vibrant and alive. It indicates a strong personality developed over many life-times which is available for the use of spirit (his higher self). Alas, his ego-mind has other *ideas* which are focused, not on spirit's expression of love and joy upon the earth, but on goals of achievement and self-esteem.

Ideas, then, are what is blocking integration here. The exclusivity of his *ideas* are excluding the feelings he is living in denial of. The body happens to have a sensitive barometer within it which, whilst it cannot talk to you, can let you know by feelings what spirit desires of you. Yet, many so-called spiritual people cannot believe the body can teach them anything. They deny its part in the whole. They cannot believe that anything as "gross" as the body can be linked to spirit or have anything to teach them. They ignore it and they deny its intelligence. They look instead to heaven, to what they think is upward and uplifting. But they look in the wrong place. Within them, within the very body they despise and ill treat are the very clues and messages which, if listened to, if understood, *and acted upon*, open the door to heaven on earth. There is no other heaven on earth, other than that which you are experiencing for your self in your own personal, physical, body, *right NOW*. Your body is your "earth". It can also be your heaven. It is the key part of your whole Self which you are denying. Embrace it and bring it, with love, into your consciousness. Use its keys. Listen to its intelligence.

You know, you can attune to(and listen to) your spirit by using your body like the radio receiver that it is. Trust it and become whole. Trust the joy in your body. Let visions fade away. Allow your "doing" to come naturally out of your "being". Let there be heaven on earth. This, then, is to be your goal: to have the goal of a visionless vision. It is none other than the Oneness dancing in the body. Feel it and honour it.

Let your heart, not your head, lead you. End dreams and fantasies. End control. Find your life in each moment. Awaken to song, dance and laughter. Go beyond self-consciousness.

27. THE MAN WITH OPEN ARMS.
(Surrender).

A man, bared to the waist, stands astride with open arms. He is looking up.

Nothing in life, whether it be upon a spiritual path or not, is achieved without surrender. We surrender our childhood when we move into adolescence. We surrender adolescence when moving into adulthood. With maturity, we surrender our dreams, our beliefs, our long held attitudes that have been dear to us for so long, realising they are not the source of our happiness. We surrender control, by letting go what we believed was best for our loved ones, or what we had to do about our enemies, or for the peoples of the world, or for our environment. We surrender, at the last, to all knowing - to all the opinions, concepts and roles that gave us our sense of identity. And, of course, one day, we surrender up our physical body to return to planes of existence which are more fluid and have an immeasurably faster vibratory response than the physical world: the seemingly limitless non-physical levels of *being*. Indeed, it's all about letting-go.

All this surrender could well make us exhausted. Indeed, if we fight it, it does. The more we hold on, refusing to acknowledge what is after all a natural process, the more exhausting and bewildering it all becomes. Life becomes a joy-less existence racked with grief and suffering. We feel burdened, cynical, bitter or apathetic. The aim of all this letting-go, however, is not to leave you bereft of nourishment or support or to weaken your personality. It is simply to reveal to the personality, which believes itself to be separate, its illusory nature. Such limiting beliefs, being held through many life-times, are held in place by nameless unconscious fears, by many nameless dreads, terrors and stifling guilt.

It is these beliefs that keep you in thrall to the forces of materialism to which you have become addicted; seeing nothing else, so coming to believe in nothing else, living by instinct rather than by intuition and awareness.

The aim is not to do away with the personality. Personality is the gift of Oneness to all created creatures. The more you love it, treasure it, develop it, use it, the greater your beauty. Your skills, your insights, are not lost. Your personality is your coat of many colours beautifully developed and matured over many lives, perhaps in many worlds. It is yours. It is your achievement, and joy is to be found in every colour. *You will never lose it.* What you are required to lose are the fears and limiting beliefs that presently surround it and prevent your personality being fused with your spirit (your Higher Self) and the Oneness. In the process of surrendering these beliefs and fears, it may seem like the end of your personality, yet this is just another fear. It is not so. You find to your amazement you have not "died" after all. In fact, you are more alive and more your self than ever!

When surrender is required, a good way of looking at it is to offer up what is surrendered to God (the Oneness), giving it back from whence it came. This makes your gift sacred. There is no loss, only release and expansion. At the end of all doing, at the end of all hope, you will stand like the man in this card, confidently astride the world, your loins girded (note the belt about his sex centre).

The scarf which twines around his body, up to his head, indicates control of the lower nature and a raising up of energy to the higher centres. Open hearted, arms flung wide, holding nothing - the moment being sufficient unto itself - you stand within the eternal NOW. It is both your destiny and your eternal joy.

You are required to let-go of something. Find out what it is.

28. THE TEACHER.   (Healing).

A man in a light green robe is sitting on a black tiger, striped green and blue. The tiger is crouched and alert. The man has a stick behind him. He is holding up his right hand in a blessing.

Green and blue predominate in this card. And black indicates power. It indicates that this card is to do with healing. Healing is the art of making whole. Yet, is it not truer to say: that healing is the art of removing from the person to be healed the illusory belief that they are not already whole! Wholeness, integration, harmony, and balance come about when spirit and personality (the two great opposites *which only appear to be opposite*) are reconciled. Each person on earth, whether they know it or not, is on their own personal quest for such a reconciliation.

The colours blue, indigo and violet have an affinity toward the finer energies of spirit. Red, orange and yellow (colours that, incidentally, are no less spiritual) are characteristic of the more dense energies of spirit (matter). A blending of blue and yellow gives us green. Light apple green - the green of the rainbow - is the colour of our future upon the earth. It is strikingly present in the aura of the enlightened man or woman. Globally, it will signal to the earth a return to its natural blue-green beauty. Green represents balance and harmony. It is the colour of the Christ Principle in action.

Obviously, to be the very best of help, a teacher of wholeness needs to be whole himself or herself. To become whole requires you to be fully conscious of all that has hitherto been unconscious (being the dark or invisible) in your psyche. The black tiger here represents the power of the unconscious, which is also a symbol for the Oneness, out of which all arises. The tiger's blue and green stripes, matching the colours of its rider's clothes, indicate integration. Unawareness has become awareness. New energy is available to the healer for his use. His right hand, the hand of action, blesses the world. His (Zen) stick is available (behind his left shoulder) to be used for waking up sleeping pupils! The blue scarf round his head signals that his brow chakra is awake and that his vision is a spiritual one.

This card, then, indicates a person who has achieved a large measure of integration. You are - or have the potential to be - a force for good in the world. You have within you the power to heal. Now, what is healing? How can you make whole that which is, from a spiritual perception, already whole?   Indeed, all you can do is to inspire the person to be healed to remember, and to recognise, what has already been there within him or her, all along, original, pristine and immutable. In fact, this recognition on their part can effect quite dramatic results.   It can on occasion effect instant healing which can well become permanent if that recognition is maintained and crystallised in the personality as self-realisation. The personality is not lost, but illumined by such realisation. So, we repeat that healing is not so much the art of making whole, but the art of helping another remove their belief that they are not whole. There are many ways to assist another to make this inner realisation; happily, you will be glad to hear that the devious ploys of the ego is more than matched by the skills of the army of helpers present on the physical plane today. You are one of them. In the past, religions have emphasised outer worship toward God or a prophet. This will change as it is understood that it is only the relinquishment of all beliefs, total elimination of self-consciousness, and surrender to the God of love and joy within, which brings heaven on earth.

You are required to relinquish all concerns of self and of healing to the Universe. Relinquishment is faith in action. Go forth and heal in the manner that most brings joy to your heart.

29. THE PEASANT WARRIOR. (Simplicity).

A man in simple brown apparel, wearing a helmet, is walking. He has a green stave under his left arm and is looking to his right.

Not everyone in the world is willing, or, indeed, ready to embark upon the search which leads to self-realisation. There will always be people whom you know who will not have the slightest desire in this direction - and be even less interested in hearing about it. This should not concern us. Everyone is an aspect of God (The Oneness), whether they know it or not, and does not God have the right to be what he or she wishes and to do or experience whatever he or she wishes to experience?

That is not to say, we cannot to object to the behaviour of others if we are so moved. Of course, we can! To do otherwise would be for us to live in denial. Yet, it is not for us to impose our will on how we think others should live their lives. We may suggest, inspire, encourage and, best of all, set an example. But impose our will? Absolutely not. And remember, we were given legs: we can, like the man in this card, always walk away!

How can we know what is good for others when most of us don't even trust in what is good for ourselves. There has surely been enough meddling already in our own life. We don't need to add to it by meddling in the lives of others. Especially within our immediate family! Remember, one of the most difficult things in life is to allow those we love to be foolish (or make mistakes). We are arrogant if we believe we know what is best for others, especially when they have obviously set their heart on another course of action. Suggestions such as : "You must do this because it says so in the Bible", or suggestions that you have a special link to God or the Masters or have some superior wisdom, is spiritual arrogance. It is all nonsense. Don't argue with these people. It will get you no where. Vote with your legs. Just remove yourself and your energy from their sphere of influence. At least, you will have discovered where not to look and how not to be. Remember, also, where laughter abides, arrogance cannot be. Where laughter cannot be, do not you be either. Walk away, or - even better - run for your life.

Here, in this card, is simplicity and blissful ignorance - though it may not be all that *blissful*! Nonetheless, this man is happy with his lot and has no desire to change it. And why should he? His earthy coloured clothes show us he is close to the world. The helmet or cowl over his head shows that he is deaf to all overtures from his spirit. But no matter, his green stave indicates his youthfulness. He is looking to the right: into the world of action. Action is where his experience lies. Action in the outer world. Not meditation or contemplation, or any inner work. This is his choice. Children experience this stage in life. It is as it should be. If you meddle with his life you will frustrate him or make him angry. By interfering, you may take him away from his lesson for this lifetime. In fact, you may, unknowingly, compromise any moves he might be making toward spiritual progress, and so delay his progress.

Equally, this card may represent false simplicity, or false humility, which is arrogance disguised. Awareness is needed. It brings about a natural simplicity. When all ideas (beliefs) fall away, what is left? It is the very essence of yourself. Your IS-ness. These are your roots. This is your origin. *YOU remain*, eternally. In true simplicity there is peace. Your compassion for all of life is now boundless. You have realised one-ness. There is nothing more simple than ONE.

End your preoccupation with the affairs of others. You are not going toward greater energy but toward the simplicity of peace.

30. THE RICH MAN.   (Money).

A dark skinned man, wearing a dark green velvet cloak and red trousers, is riding a bright blue dog-dragon. He is holding a weapon in his left hand. On his head he is wearing a silver circlet fashioned into the heads of two snakes.

Here we have a person who is devoting their energy to the making of money. A powerful personality is indicated (note the pugnacious visage of both master and dragon). The brilliant blue colour of this dog-like dragon shows that this entity's spirit (sky) energy is well grounded upon the earth. People who are "well earthed" usually find it easy to make money and increase their wealth. That this is not necessarily a recipe for happiness is obvious. See his sullen expression. Yet, the reverse is just as true, for, neither does poverty necessarily open a magic door to enlightenment or self-realisation.

As in all things, balance is the magic key to bring about harmony in a system - whether that system be a planetary system or a personality. So, here we have to look at denial. Denial of deeply buried feelings - fears and insecurities - leads to form addiction and consequential emotional miseries. Denial of form, or the belittling of form in favour of spirit, leads to spiritual arrogance, and a cold heart, which gives rise to feelings of isolation and much mental and emotional agony. Both give rise to disease in the body. It is common for both to be present at the same time. Integration of the apparent opposites of form and spirit brings about a respect for both, an attachment to neither, and a re-birth into something new.

Those living in denial will often make a virtue out of making money. To salve their conscience they will then give it away. This gives them standing in the community. Compulsive money makers create wealth for a variety of reasons: security, power, recognition, self-esteem, self-indulgence, sex, and so on. But behind this compulsion, as in all addictions, lies *fear;* the fear of being alone, of being unloved, or of not having, of not achieving, or of not existing. These are deep rooted fears. They are the challenges that meet all entities who visit earth. And why do entities come here? To meet these challenges, of course, here on the physical plane - the plane of demonstration and final actualisation - and to prove to themselves that these tired old fears are indeed illusory. In proving this to their satisfaction, they become "masters" of the universe; liberated from it, yet remaining in it as loving co-creators. Tibetans call them the Dragons of Wisdom.

The shadow side to the love of riches (note his dark skin) is signalled in this card. Sadly, this man is a master, not of wholeness, but of duality. Note: not one serpent, but twin serpents are raised upon his brow. Unless this man puts his material wealth to good use: for self-discovery and healing, this will be a wasted life-time. Those who exploit the earth for material gains leave an arid waste behind them. But the real waste is the aridity in themselves. His left hand (his feminine aspect) is holding a powerful looking bludgeon. He is prepared to override his feelings in his implacable pursuit of materialistic ends. His God is money, control and security. He puts it before spiritual, or ethical, human values. Feelings are in denial. There is a need here to put the material world into perspective, and to release fear into emotion.

This card calls for a deep probing of the meaning of profit and loss in your life. What reality are you creating for yourself?

31. THE FLYING SAGE.
(Spiritual Pride).

A wise old man, wearing a green robe, is sitting on a stork, looking toward the ground. He is grasping his beard in his left hand. In his right hand he holds a staff. The bird has its feet out, ready to land, and is looking to its left.

This card speaks to us of a person who has knowledge and is advanced upon the spiritual path. In China the stork is a symbol of longevity. Indeed, this person has found a measure of harmony in his life (the green robe). He has learned to fly (freedom) but is still uncertain about his wings. Neither he nor the bird look comfortable. He looks as if he might take a tumble at any moment. The stoic expression on the old man's face suggests he has made sacrifices but they haven't made him particularly happy. The tight band about his bald head bulging with brains denotes his preoccupation with his own "spiritualised" opinions, and the constriction which this limitation will have upon his psyche. In other words, he is in love with his own wisdom. He is addicted to knowledge for knowledge's sake.

This is a mind in love with the brilliance of itself. Alas, for some people knowledge is as addictive as any narcotic. Self-realisation, however, is not to be found through mental analysis, nor through secret knowledge, and certainly not through these cards! - in fact, not by anything you can *do or learn*. It comes through grace when you are receptive, when you have, in fact, finished all that you can do. It is the way of the heart. The left hand of this old soul, however, has a firm grasp on his beard (the Chinese symbol of wisdom). He is holding on to wisdom. It is his security blanket. Why? Because it makes him appear dignified. He enjoys being mysterious and devious, and making an impression. His stave in his right hand shows that he is a sage. He has moved beyond many desires - but perhaps he has not quite yet gone beyond spiritual ones, nor gone beyond his reliance on his image in his chosen role as a wise old sage. Otherwise, why should he be holding on so tightly to his stave? Who needs to hold on to anything if you are truly flying ?

This person is at that difficult stage where much progress has been made, many life-times lived, much letting go achieved and much knowledge has been obtained along the way. Glimpses of enlightenment (flying) have been seen. Yet, integration and at-onement is still around the corner. It is difficult to fly when your head is full of ideas about how to fly. To fly is not to dismiss the earth as an uncomfortable reality to rise above. It is to embrace the earth (and your physical body) at the same time as surrendering control of your life to your spirit. See how the sage and the bird are looking in different directions. Indeed, the stork (his spirit), attempting to land upon the earth, is looking to the left (to the feminine side) whilst the sage, longing to fly but afraid to fly, is still looking somewhat anxiously at the ground, in fear of fear of falling.

A desire for things spiritual combined with a tendency to elevate knowledge to sacred status, or as a device to seek the ultimate, gives rise to subtle frustrations and insecurities. You have done much work. You are much loved, helpful, and compassionate towards others. But a fall, and a hard one, is always a possibility. However, good fortune! You hold the key to the door. Don't delay in using it!

It is time to surrender all your knowing. Become a child again. Relax into your heart and find your joy. Listen to your spirit and fly.

32. THE MAN OF SKULLS.
(Superstition).

A man with large elfin ears and masses of red hair has seven skulls hanging around his neck. In his left hand he carries a sword. His right hand is stretched downward in a grasping motion.

This man has a distinctly primitive look about him. His footwear and apparel indicate simple living. His pointed elf-like ears indicate he is attuned to nature. Yet, his sprouting red hair, his necklace of skulls and grasping right hand tell a different story.

It is as well to remember that merely being close to nature does not automatically mean you are a loving person. There are certain primitive tribes on earth who may seem, by modern day urban standards, to have an idyllic life-style, being simple and close to nature. Yet, the peoples of these tribes are besieged by fear. They fear the witch-doctor, the lawman, and a whole pantheon of unseen spirits. Tribal law, *taboo* and magic, rule. Women are possessions to be bartered in marriage. Mutilation of body parts is common. So-called morality disadvantages women. Witchdoctors and lawmen control their subjects by dire threats of punishment and misfortune (alas, as does the Catholic Church and Islam even today). Bad spirits or going against God's laws are conveniently blamed for being the cause behind illness and natural disasters. This is all gross superstition. Born out of ignorance, it generates fear, which then feeds on more fear. Reality and illusion become hopelessly blurred and entangled.

The only thing to benefit from this muddle is, of course, our old friend the conditioned ego - that curious separate identity that we humans make for our self, believing it to be the true self. Fear, and primitivism, combine with nature (and religious maniacs) to make a potent brew. This stew pot throws up dire illusions for the gullible to be ensnared by.

To have an empathy with nature is a fine thing. It can teach you much. Indeed, it may be essential to be with nature many times in your life in order to de-contaminate yourself from urban conditioning or other social factors, to seek your own stillness within. These can be important times. However, it is quite another thing to become so attracted to nature and all its marvels that it becomes another addiction. The forms of nature are fascinating. Yet, they can become too fascinating. Yes, of course, do love and cherish nature. Yes, there are other streams of evolution sharing this earth with us. But nature is not to be worshipped. The Greek god *Pan* (a figure born out of nature-worship) is a magically personified thought-form of illusion for the unwary. The bountiful gifts of our "mother earth" need not be an entrapment. They are merely bountiful gifts. See them as such and don't put the mind to ought else. Beware the skulls around your neck. They are born out of superstition. They rattle emptily to the tune of death.

Worship and superstition - and fear - go hand in hand. They prevail in every religion on earth today. Priests foster (in their ignorance) this unholy alliance; but it all began - it had its origins - in early times of tribal nature-worship. Nothing you will ever do and no God you will ever worship, or fear, can ever change the intrinsic fact that this universe is a universe of love and joy. So, maybe I can make a small suggestion. Relax! Laugh! Dance! Sing! And trust in your innermost feeling of who you are! Be original. Be unique. Be YOU. BE HERE NOW. Say a big NO to all that has gone before. A big NO to superstition! A big NO to religions!

You have nothing to prove to anyone - least of all to God, to any guru, or to any religious authority. Love yourself into Life.

33. THE ZEN MASTER.   (Yang).

A man in a blue robe is leaning to his left. He has a small crown with a red tassel on his head. In his right hand, draped over his shoulder, is a fly whisk. There is a red and black symbol on his sleeve. His left hand is open in a blessing.

The ***Tao Te Ching*** says that everything in manifestation, whether on the physical plane as we know it or existing in a higher vibratory realm, has a form. Even creatures of pure mind have a form. Consciousness cannot exist without form, however tenuous.

All forms, however subtle, (including thought forms), have an affinity toward the material, the mother, *the yin*, side of existence. This is very natural and as it should be. Now, the active principle of motivating energy (spirit) which informs matter is seen, therefore, as *the yang* or male element (note his blue robe). Everything in existence reflects to a greater or lesser degree one or other of these two great principles, *yin* or *yang*. Human beings also reflect them, not only in their physical forms, but in their emotions and minds. Now, the integration of both these two elements (the yin and the yang) within *all the vehicles* of human personality, *with spirit,* is necessary before an entity can take its place in a wider sphere of influence in the universe.

Personality has an affinity toward either *yin* or *yang* through which the personality will express itself. This card depicts the *yang* expression of such a personality. So, how does *yang*-ness express itself through humans? As *yang* has an affinity toward spirit, it is evident that *yang* itself is not so much the doer, but the energy *behind* all doing. Such a man, therefore, is not so much a creator but the power behind creativity. He is not so much a carer but the love (and energy) that IS behind all caring acts (as in compassion). He is not so much the wise guru but the truth and awareness which lies behind all wisdom. Thus we see, in fact, that the true *yang* expression is not an outer one of creativity in the world of matter, but an inner one of *being* in the world of matter. It is, in other words, responsive to energy *within* the world of matter without being entangled in it or enslaved by it. We see that it is the male role *to be* the loving energy of spirit, whilst it is the female role *to use it* (using creative mind). This doesn't mean that males cannot be creative, or that females cannot be joyful and spontaneous in their loving. Wholeness contains within it all the elements. But it does mean that those with a strong *yang* affinity (not necessarily having a male sex body) should be aware that they are here on earth mainly to be the carriers of loving energy, rather than the users of it. They are here to be lovers, joy bringers, inspirers - to be examples of "love in action", rather than knowing what action to take. They are here to give of their loving energy to those *yin* entities whose role it is to disseminate knowledge, to teach, to heal, and to care for the earth. The *yin* brings meaning to existence, the *yang* brings joy to meaning. When a woman trusts her own spirit, her male partner may act as a conduit for spiritual energy which, combined with hers, may give rise to wondrous creative powers.

In a balanced partnership, where there is mutual trust, a woman's vision and a man's energy, can manifest a powerful expression of love in action on the physical plane. Thus, the *yin* and the *yang* work together on the physical plane - and on every plane - mutually supportive of each other.

The challenge here is to explore and to accept your male side. It may very well be opposite to what you have been brought up to believe. Honour your feelings, especially those of love denied. Guard the mind.

34. THE SNAKE WOMAN. (Yin)

A beautiful woman, with the body of a blue snake from the waist down, is dressed in a simple pink robe. She has her arms folded and gazes gently toward the ground.

As opposed to the *yang* (see Card 33), the *yin* element in existence has an affinity with all forms. It creates them. It destroys them. Mind is the mother of form. Out of its own substance it creates thought forms. When clothed with emotion and a physical body, and prompted by the energy of the indwelling spirit, a personality develops. This personality may temporarily forget its origin (spirit) and go off on its own separatist way on many adventures in many form worlds before remembering its source. It is the mind that has this mercurial ability to construct for itself endless forms, endless illusions, endless dreams, endless hypotheses, and endless adventures and challenges which can keep a separatist-minded soul endlessly entertained (and ensnared) for many aeons and many life-times.

However, just as you can "set a thief to catch a thief", so can you - by inviting your mind to be a detached observer and training it in the art of discernment - use your mind to peel away the illusions, the attitudes and beliefs, which keep you ignorant of your source (the Oneness). Ignorance of, or denial of, our spirit, is the cause of all suffering. Our source is love. It is our very being. It is, in fact, the root of all consciousness. Everything that exists has consciousness in it: sticks and stones, mud and mountains, beetles, trees, fish, the clouds and the wind, everything. All is informed with loving consciousness. Individualised consciousness, as in humans - and some cetaceans - brings with it the gift of self-awareness and the possibility of a fully conscious fusion with spirit.

The *(yin)* energies within form are powerful energies. They need to be in order to hold it all together and create more of it. In the case of humans, these energies can be harnessed for creativity. Yet, if creativity is at the expense of forgetting your origin and feeling separate from your source, fear enters in and suffering follows. On the other hand, your *yin* energies can be invited to re-unite with your spirit. This is enlightenment. When, within you, your knowledgeable mind - which you are no longer attached to - unites with your love (*yang* or truth), wisdom reigns. To be a dragon of wisdom is your goal. And, remember, dragons may be fearsome and breathe fire but they also love to dance!

First, loving acceptance of self is necessary (the gentle pink). Harmlessness (note her covered hands) and simplicity (note her sparse adornments) is also required. The energies of the physical body (without being suppressed or denied) must be invited to carry a higher frequency - frequencies that no longer support elements of fear or anxiety. You decide to do nothing that does not nourish you. This is not being selfish. This is being self-aware. This is your destiny. This acceptance of everything about yourself. Irrespective of whether you are in a male or female sex body, you need to become becomes the ultimate in receptivity (*yin*). It leads to acceptance (another word for love) of everything outside of you. You become an open vessel. A personality open to spirit. And spirit is not long in responding!

Be more receptive (which is not to be passive!). Live without guile. Accept your "shadow self" and use its energies (emotions) to open your heart and live life more vibrantly. Love your body, trust in your spirit, and watch your mind.

35. THE VIOLET MAN.　(Therapy).

A man in a violet robe is holding a bagua (a Chinese bell) in his left hand. Over his right shoulder he has a fly whisk. He has a flame coming from a gold band round the centre of his head. There are three design motifs on his robe: a snake, a mandala and seven stars.

This card, which applies equally, of course - as all these cards do - to a female master, represents a teacher who comes from the stars (note the seven stars of the Pleiades constellation). He or she is a master of the energies that lie within form (the golden snake). That these energies are under the direction of his spiritual self is indicated by the fire blazing from his third eye centre. The mandala over his solar plexus (personality) centre, with its eight rays (denoting infinity), is a galactic symbol. This entity is of extra-terrestrial origin who has taken human form. His skills are available to all who are drawn to him. The bagua is a Taoist symbol of prophecy, of a seer. He has a bell to ring. Those who have the wisdom to hear of him will do so.

What skills is he offering? His violet robe is the clue. His particular interest is *transformation*. The fiery, red and yellow, sleeves to his arms show that his activity is in the use of the fiery energies within matter. He knows how to use ritual to assist in the dissolution of old attitudes, beliefs and fears. He brings about integration in those he helps. He encourages humans to remember their source and trust in spirit. He helps them to love themselves more, to love others more, to be loved more, *to be more*. It's all about love. This is the work of transformation. This is therapy. And it starts with loving yourself more. Nothing is more important.

So what is therapy? Therapy is the art of helping a person to become conscious of that which has hitherto been unconscious, and to integrate the energy thus released into a new way of being which more accurately expresses their essence vibration. This is spiritual growth.

It entails facing and letting go of limiting attitudes and negative belief systems. It usually means changing a self-defeating life-style for one that *nourishes you with higher feelings - especially those feelings of love and joy and peace.* It means devoting close attention to feelings at the expense of mind constructs, which, for the moment, need to be set aside. Deep feelings, long suppressed or denied, under the guidance of a skilled master therapist, need to be brought into the light of day and honoured, so that the energy locked up in them can be released and be available for use in a more satisfying everyday life. Contrary to what the priests of earthly religions believe, this, and not worshipping, or the chanting of prayers, to a saviour or prophet or guru, *or God*, is spiritual work.

It is this clearing out of old fears, terrors and anxieties, the confronting and releasing of old conditioning that reconnects you with your spirit. This is life affirming. This is love affirming. This is joy and peace affirming. This is balancing. And it is real spiritual work. A great secret, long suppressed on this planet (by those who would control you),is that feelings nourish. The higher feelings of love and joy nourish and affirm your Higher Self. Lower feelings of fear and passion nourish the instinctual form life. Whichever way you look at it, feelings, are, in truth, the universal nourishment. God-like feelings is the food of the gods - and food *for the gods*. It is your food. You need to recall who you are and regain that which nourishes you. It may mean saying NO to those who would keep you starved. A big beautiful **NO!**

Your surrender, for a while, to the skills of a master therapist is indicated here. You need to face deep and long held fears.

70

36. A MAN ON A DEER. (Change).

*A man, simply dressed in a dark robe, is sitting on a flower-patterned red deer. The trigrams on his cloak represent the yin/yang symbols from the **I Ching**.*

One of the most ancient books in China is the Book of Changes, the **I Ching.** It is still in use today as a guide to spiritual growth and for divination in every day matters. In the trigrams the lines are either firm and unbroken, *yang* lines; or broken and yielding, *yin lines.* In the ancient teachings an initiate was likened to a deer. He or she needed to be alert, sensitive and fleet of foot. Every year the deer sheds, then grows new antlers. We all need to shed old beliefs, old attitudes, old fears, and alter our life-style to accommodate our new awareness. This is an on-going process. There are said to be five stages (rites of passage) or "initiations" that humans go through on earth on their path to illumination and self-realisation. At the first initiation there is mastery over the basest desires of the physical body; the heart begins to open. A first glimpse of life's true purpose is given and understood. The second initiation forms a crisis in the appreciation of, and control of(but not repression or denial of) the emotions. At the third initiation, the personality is flooded with light as the mind is enthusiastically harnessed in the work of service in the world; to which end a vision is shown of what lies ahead. The fourth initiation is one of sacrifice, entailing the letting go of all personality ideas of your role and identity, and, maybe, friends, money, reputation, character, even life itself. All is renounced. All is offered up to the fires of transformation. It is a time of anguish and hardship, yet a time to be endured for it need not last long if entered into *totally* with integrity, awareness and humility. The Fifth human initiation is that of self-realisation. Initiations after the fifth move into the realm of planetary or solar experience, or beyond.

The earth (being the physical body of a sentient entity) is now preparing for His and Her imminent solar initiation. Humanity, however, living on the earth and within the auric field of this entity, is very busy preparing for its first initiation. You who read these words may be a more senior initiate here to help. At times of change there is always plenty of help at hand. This is very true today. And your help is needed.

After self-realisation, changes still continue; new experiences are offered, responsibilities widen; but with the difference that there is no more separation. Each initiation has to be gone through afresh in each lifetime; but if it has been taken in a previous life it is quickly passed and often barely noticed. Spirit loves to keep mobile; experiencing greater and greater realities. Change is the means by which this happens. Change is a constant factor in life. One might say, change *is* life. Change allows a space to open up in your life where something new - where something *more* - can happen. It doesn't have to be physical, yet again it may need to be. Change happens primarily in consciousness. Joy is to be found in the spaces of life. So, when you have a choice as to which direction to go, choose the path which, above all, nourishes greater feelings within you of joy and excitement. Let the "joy of your being" be your compass. Martial your courage. Love yourself enough *to have the strength of will to honour your own god within*. Do not pander to what others want. It may perhaps seem selfish, but fear not: it will be *your* path toward self-realisation; *your* path to a more abundant life. To change is to go forward. To refuse to change is to be left behind in a dark room.

Embrace change. Get used to it and welcome it. It is your friend.

37. THE MERCHANT.　(Passivity).

A man in a dark velvet coat, arms folded, stares at the ground. He is wearing a bejewelled hat and a blue collar round his neck.

Yes, life is meant to be easy. But, hopefully, this is an easiness that comes from knowing who you are; standing in your own light and doing what is yours to do. False easiness is a pretence. It is a cover up. It is a game of the fearful ego, which would rather not look into its unconscious for fear of how it might be affected. And thus, fears and denied feelings are never dealt with. If you have money, somewhere to live, a little entertainment to keep you from being completely bored, why bother to make the effort to deal with fears? Why? Because, if you don't, you will slide into *passivity*. This soon become laziness, opening the door to resentment and cynicism; which will soon hang around you like a dark cloud and dominate your feeling life. It will become a burden about your shoulders (note the hunched over bearing of the man in this card). In your outer face to the world you project ease and confidence, but you are not truly at ease. You are a master (a merchant) of compromise. You let nothing affect you because you yield to anything that might threaten. You agree to anyone who might argue. You lose in order to win. But it is not natural. It is a mind manipulation, because *you do really want to be top dog!* This is a subtle game called "passive aggression". It can fool people at first meeting but is not sustainable, for, sooner or later, you will have your bluff called - and now you have to become even more passive! Resentment builds. You further isolate yourself in your carefully constructed facade of easiness. Life may take on a dream-like quality about it. You wallow in it. Through thick and thin you hold it together. But in your inner life you are seething with frustration. Life is no longer so easy!

This man is full of wonderful ideas about himself but (like his jewel encrusted hat) they are all in his head. His unconscious (see his dark robe), is like a sponge full of hidden fears, soaking up his emotional energy. His physical life is not receiving the energy it requires to function with any sense of natural aliveness or creativity (note his hands are clenched and hidden). This man is trading away real aliveness - which might have some physical or emotional danger in it - for a stagnant, easy, life. He has no wish (no will) to confront his fears. Maybe he would like to change but the reality of it frightens him. He is not prepared to make himself vulnerable enough to find out. He has no wish to push himself, or place himself, in any situation where he might be forced to admit to inner terror. He uses his clever mind to wriggle out of every tricky situation. He creates nothing for himself but reacts only to whatever life brings. In fact, he is anti-life. The blue collar round his neck reminds one of an upside down *ankh;* the ancient Egyptian symbol of *life.* But here it is inverted, strangling him.

In his inaugural speech, in 1994, in one of the greatest speeches of all time, Nelson Mandela said: *"Our deepest fear is not that we are inadequate. Our deepest fear is that we are powerful beyond measure. It is our light not our darkness that most frightens us.....Your playing small doesn't serve the world. There is nothing enlightened about shrinking so that other people won't feel insecure around you. We are born to manifest the glory of god that is within us."*

Your throat centre (chakra) is your centre for sounding forth your "word" (your note and vibrational frequency). From it you self-create your self. This is a very loving universe; wholly accepting. Whatever you wish to see yourself as, it will agree to. It will accept anything you wish to be, or do. If you give fear a snug home and live in pretence, it will accept it, still loving you (albeit, whilst confronting you from time to time by your fear). If you truly want to be attuned to your spirit, to the Oneness and your Higher Self, it will agree to the extent of opening doors for you. If you want to be a teacher or a healer, or a bringer of joy, and live in truth as a master - walking upon the earth as a Dragon of Wisdom, it will accept that also. It is all up to you.

Be ruthlessly honest with your feelings. Shine your light.

38. THE FAT MAN.   (Greed).

A fat man clothed in many colours is standing with his feet astride, head thrown back. He has a money belt attached to a dark red apron round his middle. He has a flat-board hat on his head.

This man is at home in his body. Indeed, this is his problem: he is too much at home. He has become self-important, self-satisfied and self-indulgent. In other words, it's all to do with self, self, self. Behind all this pre-occupation with self - and we are talking here about the conditioned ego - is the greedy mind. And why is his mind so greedy? Because of deep and chronic fear. He has become attached (addicted) to security. So, he is fat; the more flesh surrounding him the better. All the better to insulate him from needing *to feel*. And how does this come about? Because, at some time, either in this life time or in a past life, he was deeply hurt emotionally. And, at that very time, he decided it would not happen again. So, now, he shuts himself off from anything that might remind him of those past feelings. Now, in his present day life, he denies that such feelings might even exist - or are in any way useful. He is living in "denial". He has shut off his link to spirit.

But, and it is such a huge BUT, your feelings *(by way of your intuition) are the most direct link you have to your spirit.* Yes, the reasoning, logical, mind has its part to play, of course; but NOT as the receiver of spirit's desires. This is not its role. It cannot even do it. Your intuition is designed to do this, and must be developed to do this. Your reasoning mind's role is marvellously functional and creative. It is very good at it. It is very bad, however, at understanding your *need to feel*.

Now, using your intuition to access your spirit, your feelings light up. Your feelings, lit by spirit, then enthuse (illuminate) your mind with the energy required to get a job done (let us say, your earth mission!). Thus all is in balance and all goes along according to spirit's plan of wholeness rather than the elitist ego's desperate plan of power, control and partiality. Feelings are your all-important link to spirit. And they are your soul's nourishment. So, above all, honour them and trust them, learn to love and enjoy them, and live with them. If you learn nothing else in this life time, learn this. It is the key to everything.

This man's flat hat shows that he is making a clear decision to separate himself from his spirit. His intuition has become an irrelevancy in his life. He is sheltering in the comfortable shade of his conditioned mind (his ego). He is obese with good living. His fat girth is a subtle armour which absorbs his finer feelings, allowing him to ignore and keep his deeper, unconsciously denied, feelings well hidden. Rather than a soft golden glow coming from his solar plexus (his personality centre), blessing the world with the radiance of his love, his money belt bulges forth like a dark cancer from his stomach, protecting it and feeding it. His contentment is to be short-lived.

Greed is characteristic of a mind that is forced to take ever increasing steps to shore up a demanding and increasingly fearful ego under threat from unconscious fears. Inevitably, like the rocks of an island surrounded by a relentless sea, the ego will one day crumble. To fight this is to prolong suffering. To accept it is to open the door to joy.

Become aware of your mind and its greed. Develop your intuition, listen to your spirit and trust in your feelings. Trust that whatever comes is the perfect opportunity for you to go beyond greed.

39. THE MAN WITH NO HANDS.
(Harmlessness).

A man in a blue robe, with gold under garment, and pink apron, is standing, staring at the ground. His hands are hidden beneath the sleeves of his robe.

Harmlessness is an almost forgotten art; but for anyone who wishes to progress on the spiritual path it is of supreme importance. It is another word for acceptance, and acceptance is another word for love. Learning *Self*-acceptance is the essential prerequisite for acceptance of everything outside of yourself. Harmlessness and love walk hand in hand. When your mind is harmless, love is automatically there. Indeed, *love is creativity that is sufficient unto itself.* From the view point of enlightened entities, creativity doesn't mean creating more masterpieces. Of course, you cannot create love, for love already IS. But you can create an environment for it to arise in and be recognised. You can be a loving home maker. A loving employer. You can be a caring environmentalist, legislator or politician. You can be a loving and inspirational musician, artist, or heart-warming writer. You can be a loving councillor, or a loving therapist who helps people to get in touch with their feelings. You can be a loving example of new ways, perhaps - an inspirational "destroyer" of old attitudes and beliefs, a stirrer of stagnant emotion, or of old feelings long denied which are now wishing to move. Remember, when emotion moves, life moves. Beliefs which are no longer useful for the evolution of your indwelling life will suffocate you. Anyone who confronts you with this fact, painful though it might be, is pressing your buttons and pricking your ego, bringing to your attention an area to be worked on. If this is done with good will and without conscious desire to harm, then it is harmless. A truly loving act.

Because of the many old ghosts (the unrecognised fears) which remain in the unconscious, all are involved in this work from time to time. Some find themselves involved in it constantly. This is their mission on earth. They break up old patterns of behaviour. They provoke, stir up, confront, and generally break up the old so that the new can come in. It is valuable work. But it must come out of harmlessness and not out of a desire to convert someone to your way of thinking or believing! Remember, the real Self, the real You, cannot be harmed. Anything that releases you from your outer mask (the conditioned ego-personality) is a loving act.

To be harmless is not to be passive. It is to be clear seeing, looking always to the life beneath the form and serving its needs. Harmlessness requires you to honour your feelings, to keep your emotion flowing, your life energy moving, and accept it all. It requires you to accept everything that the outside brings you, whilst at the same time standing in your own light, knowing that it brings you opportunity for more spiritual growth. You have your own special part to play in the connectedness of everything that goes to make up this world. You are designed for that part and no other. You are unique. Feel this. Know this. God (the Oneness) designed you this way and no other way *for a reason*. You are very much loved; very much needed. This is self-acceptance. This is loving. This is to be harmless.

Become aware of your aggression. See how it is covered up by activity that is neither loving of yourself or of others.

40. THE MAN-WOMAN.   (Balance).

A young warrior of indeterminate gender is riding a blue dragon. Dressed in pink and violet, he/she is holding out two hammers, perfectly balanced, in each hand. Shoulders and thighs are covered with golden armour.

What a beautiful card this is. Here we have a liberated master, one of the Dragons of Wisdom so beloved of ancient China and Tibet. This the legendary *Er Lang,* who has come down from heaven to confront the Monkey King (conditioned mind). This is an androgynous entity (note the blue and green dragon) in harmony with spirit. Soul quality is indicated by pink and violet. The golden armour around the shoulders (are they not like angels' wings?) and covering his or her thighs, indicate that this youthful entity can *fly* (is enlightened) and has an abundantly responsive and sensitive (but not sexual) nature. Please note, the key word here is *responsive,* not responsible! The weapons (the hammers) indicate balance and strength.

Here we have a bringer of gifts to the world. What better gift to bring than the gift of inspired *will* - being the courage to confront illusion. This master brings you the message of balance. To be truly balanced is to be appropriate to your current situation. It is not being smugly satisfied that your aggressive behaviour can exist side by side with your loving side. It is not a question of obnoxious behaviour being balanced-out by caring behaviour. It is not seeing that there is both good and bad in the world, calling it "in balance" when, in reality, it is in division.

Balance comes, not from weighing up the light and the dark, or good or bad, it comes from accepting both the opposites *and then going beyond them.* In embracing the opposites, then going beyond, something new is born. Liberation. Having embraced the opposites, you are now free of them in the sense that they no longer have any unconscious hold over you. You can now make unfettered choices. To be balanced, is not to attempt to balance *yin* with *yang,* or to try to change anything in particular. All energies have their place in this universe. Many liberated beings are bi-sexual. They are androgynous entities. Within themselves they have embraced all the opposites, including those of *yin* and *yang,* being the twin flames of consciousness. After spirit and personality fusion, sex on the physical plane is still possible but it becomes more a union of consciousness rather than the fulfilling of sexual needs. At all levels, a union of entities coming together, in love, increases the experience of love and affirms the glory of a loving creator. It is, in fact, a highly creative act because it is such an intensely total sharing. It reveals love and makes more love available. This is creation in all the worlds. You need to know that true creativity is the act of revealing more love. What work could be more worth while? Such a union is confirmation to everyone that God still exists in her and his creation, and that *love is a joy that you can actually feel in every part of it.*

Drop all your ideas of what is, or is not, in balance. They are all mind illusions. Trust your feelings and be born anew.

41. SITTING ON THE DRAGON.
(Resistance).

A man with a dark red face is sitting on a dragon. He is holding a spear in his left hand.

You get a red face when you are caught doing something you don't want others to know about. Perhaps you will even attempt to avoid owning up to it; but, nonetheless, whenever the subject is alluded to you feel threatened: you become dogmatic, stubborn, critical and - more than likely - self-righteously judgemental. You become subtly manipulative, or evasive - or fly into a rage. Yes, this will definitely give you a red face. Inside you are boiling up like a pressure cooker. A little anger might ease the pressure for the moment but provide no long term solution. When you hide your feelings for fear they will make you look weak or stupid, you are "in denial". At the very least, you are refusing to take responsibility for the less than satisfactory situation you are involved in. This is *resistance.*

The effects of resistance are legion, but it starts, of course, with our refusal to listen. And why do we refuse to listen to our spirit? Because we are afraid that if we do we are going to lose out on something. So, we hold on to that "something" like grim death. We close the door on our intuition (our link with spirit) and make a decision to subdue *feelings.* Now, intuition is the bridge between spirit and mind, so if we are to have any link with our spirit we need to use it. We need to trust it and get used to trusting it. Remember, spiritual growth is not about being a logical, or even a *reason*able, human being but becoming a *whole* human being. In fact, we need to develop our intuition in order to access more of our spirit's intentions. The more we use it the easier it becomes. After a while, it becomes so natural we wonder how we ever managed to live without it. We will have made a quantum leap into another level of consciousness.

Now, as we know, we are not essentially our mind with all its thoughts nor are we our feelings. We, the Self, are prior to these bodies which we use so we can exist as individuals on these lower planes of life. And, here, use them we must. Without feeling and without our feelings being attuned to the nourishment of our spirit, we cannot feel alive. If we don't feel alive we are not properly alive! We exist in a grey, zombie-like state, inside ourselves, perhaps existing within a comfortable ordered society - perhaps even being brilliantly creative - but, nonetheless, being depressingly, reliably, and monotonously, joyless. Our excuse might be that "life has no meaning". Yet, why should life have any meaning? If it has meaning, or doesn't have meaning, what is the problem? Life is eternal. Love is ALL. Joy is eternal. What is the problem? What other meaning are you seeking?

The problem of course is that you are still locked into your mind, demanding that life has the meaning - and only the meaning - that you, your conditioned ego, want it to have! The problem arises when we put our ultimate trust in reason and logic - and resist trusting our intuition. Instead of being nourished by the higher feelings of spirit we are nourished by feelings saturated by the instinctual energies of form. These lower feelings are feelings tainted by, and derived from, the memory of conflict and friction (violence and sex) during the evolution of form. If you choose to live by being nourished largely by lower feelings, you will be continually needing to provoke chaotic situations around you so that you can keep a supply of lower feelings available for you "to feed from". This is resistance. It is a dark path.

There is some area in your life where reason or logic is playing you false. Trust your intuition and honour feelings long denied. Look not for meaning. Seek, instead, harmony in your life.

42. THE MAN WITH THE PARASOL. (Personality).

A man is holding a parasol over his right shoulder. He is looking to the left, acting out a dance movement. He is dressed in coloured clothes with light armouring on legs and shoulders. Predominant colours are red and blue.

Are we not all actors on the stage of life? This card draws our attention to our personality, our *persona,* our mask, which we don from life-time to life-time for our chosen experience upon the earth. Yet, just as an actor in the theatre returns to his real self after being on stage, so do we return to our real Self after each life-time in the physical world.

After leaving the physical body, and after a period of healing and assessment of our recent life-time on this world, the Self we return to seems as if it might be a "higher self." However, as it turns out we are not *returning* to a higher self so much as *regaining the awareness that we are already this higher self.* It is who we are. It *is who we have always been.* It is our holistic personality - having our own personal vibrational frequency - which has always existed in a state of awareness and wholeness but which on earth we have not bothered to validate. This true Self of ours is always, and *has* always, been aware of our oneness with the All-That-Is. This Self has always been aware of all our multi-dimensional selves and aware of the links of light between all beings. Here we are aware of all our many expressions and personalities, and their experiences, both in the past and the future, in many time frames all at the same time. This is the real you. This is the Self (your Self) which experiences, constantly observing and monitoring, all that you are also experiencing. It has been called the "soul" or the "higher self" - or the "spiritual self". It is the same Self.

Your link to this great entity which is yourself is through your intuition. In listening to spirit, you are heeding the directions of your whole grand Self. But in resistance, you become so involved with (identified with), the role of your current persona that you create for yourself a separate ego (an *I*) that starts behaving in a way not previously intended by your holistic Self. Now you start believing that this earthly personality (the mask) is all you are. Alienation from your spiritual Self means alienation from your higher feelings. But, feelings are meant to nourish you. Without joy in your life your conditioned ego must look for nourishment from lower feelings *(See Card 41)*. It begins to thrive on confrontation and conflict, using reason to perpetuate a situation where love is over-ruled and friction can be maintained. For those of you, however, who are looking to become fused with your spiritual Self, lower feelings will no longer nourish you. Indeed, they will cause you acute emotional and mental anguish, which, when denied, will lead all too soon to physical collapse.

This card represents someone who is turning away from spirit (hiding under the parasol). He is looking to the left, to the past, towards form. The colours red and blue show that his vision (blue) is energised by feelings (red) emanating from form and the desire for form experience rather than from the energies of spirit (which would be green and gold). His parasol has a greenish tinge to it indicating that harmony is to be found in that direction but unfortunately that is not the direction in which he is looking.

Over identification with your personality, to the extent that it assumes for you either abhorrence or fascination, or having pride in it, is the trap to avoid here. Self-indulgent admiration of your personality is to become like *Narcissus,* the Greek *god,* who fell in love with his own reflection. This is to fall in love with illusion. It is a blind alley! But, to hate, or to blame your personality, or the denial of it, is no less an illusory state of being. You are here to follow your spirit uncompromisingly, using an earthly personality to do so. It brings you to an ever increasing realisation of the one Self which underpins (and over-lights) your personality. It leads to a natural deepening of your experience of who you truly are. It leads, of course, to greater love, to greater joy, to a profound peace and a more abundant life.

Go beyond self-consciousness. Don't take yourself so seriously. There is no higher or lower of anything. All is divine. Experience the harmony that already reigns.

43. THE MINSTREL.   (Sound).

A man with a green face, in coloured clothes, is playing a stringed instrument.

Here we have a well developed person who has found a measure of harmony (green face) in his or her life. He or she is aware of the importance of attuning to *frequency.*

Your personality can be likened to a musical instrument through which spirit breathes. Over many life-times you play your tune (undertake your missions) in many differing realities. At the moment, you are playing a human tune in this earth reality. And, in this card you are shown that spirit is sending you a message that there is much more to your present life than you can see and touch.

Everyone knows when a guitar is in tune, or out of tune. The strings are either too loose - or too tight! When in tune, you are accepting your spirit's *frequency as your own,* you begin to sing your own song. Your song will be unique to you. Whatever you choose to do, or be: a healer, teacher, artist, sage, or musician - no matter - your spiritual-self will shine through all that you do. You will be an inspiration to all you meet and, unknown to you, even the grass you tread upon will grow taller and greener as you pass by. Whatever you do, wherever you go, your healing influence will vibrate all around you. Much of this you will never know about. This is perfectly as it should be. Indeed, the more impersonal (detached from the person to be healed) is the healer from the act of healing, the more powerful the healing will be. *You do not do the healing.* You are but the channel, the vehicle, through which a *frequency* flows. This vibration is energy. It is light. It is love. It is truth. The inner life of the person to be healed recognises this frequency. The inner life is called forth in profound response to it and the healing occurs. This is resonance. You are but the catalyst through which the denial of wholeness is ended. The most profound and permanent healing is by resonance.

Your well-being depends entirely on your frequency. It never has, nor ever will, depend on what you *do* or anything you have done. You are greater by far than anything you will ever do. It is up to you to attune to your "wholeness frequency", *and maintain it.* This you do by way of your intuition and following your spirit uncompromisingly, at the expense of all other considerations. And that does mean *all other considerations!* As you adjust to this new way of living, you will begin to get the knack of it. It is not so difficult as you might think, yet there is much resistance to it on this planet from those who see nothing beyond security, sensual satisfaction, mental development and knowledge.

In the physical world, SOUND - both music and the spoken word - is a powerful conveyor of vibrational frequency. Indeed, *how you speak* is more important than what you say! Amazingly, this is true and all should take this to heart. Music - that balm to the soul - cuts across all beliefs, all religions and all ideologies. It is an intensely healing and unifying factor, yet, again, it is beneficial only if the musical frequency is harmonious and uplifting to spirit. And so it is with the words you speak. Listen, especially, to the music of your spoken words. Are they spoken with grace like unto a song that uplifts and inspires, or are they just words. Just noise. Just a noise to convey your message. Sound is the original creative impulse. You need to realise that every sound you make is a creative act, increasing love or diminishing love. This is a profound truth.

The challenge here is to start thinking of yourself as the song rather than the song-writer. Attune to your inner frequency, then bring it through into your everyday life.

44. THE SWORDSMAN.   (Fear).

A man with a red face holds aloft a sword in his right hand. He takes a fighting stance, his left arm across his body.

Humans fear so many things: fear of authority, fear of no authority, fear of not loving or of losing love, fear of loneliness, fear of lack of purpose, fear of failure, fear of sex or of not having sex, fear of nudity, fear of poverty, fear of death, fear of being different, fear of showing feelings, fear of God - and on it goes: so many anxieties. So much fear - which leads to so much shame and so much guilt over many, many life-times.

What effect does fear have on the human psyche? It contracts your aura and limits the amount of energy you have available to keep you whole and healthy. It makes you rigid, tight and inflexible. It makes you protective and defensive and, concerning that which you are particularly afraid of losing, it will make you aggressive. It makes you see red. You will fight to the death for fear of death - or even to *admitting* to a fear of death. You will avoid admitting to fear by every devious or aggressive means with all the skill of your conditioned ego.

You will never go beyond fear, however, until one bright day you can admit to it. You need to own the feelings associated with fear. You need to recognise the illusions woven around it, boldly face them, then move into a new insightful way of living where fear no longer exists. To live without fear is to live rather simply. It is to live with integrity and clarity in harmony with All-That-Is. It is to live from the realisation and utter conviction that ALL IS ONE and that you are a part of this Oneness, not as a separate particle, but as the very Oneness embodied; at the same time as understanding that you have your own unique and individual personality through which you will express the Oneness.

When fear ends, you will have a profound compassion for those still enmeshed in it. Resistance to acknowledging spirit as being your origin (your roots) and your very Self generates fear until fear becomes such a chronic and familiar way of life that, without it, you feel even more afraid. So fear generates fear and it is the fearful *mind* that keeps you going round and round in this circle. This is karma. Karma is not a tit for tat, an eye for an eye, business that you have to sort out with others. Karma is merely the next level of fear to be dealt with. You can deal with it over a long process of many life-times or you can deal with it in the twinkling of an eye. It is up to you. There is no magic formula, no religious, or mystical mumbo jumbo by which it can go away. Indeed, the solution is down to earth and practical. You must explore long denied feelings. You must discipline and watch your mind. You must honour, love and be gentle to yourself first and foremost - having respect and compassion for others. You must watch your speech, trust you intuition, follow your spirit, and allow love and joy to be your compass.

Many religions believe in the one God, but that, in itself doesn't end fear or guarantee heaven on earth - or guarantee heaven anywhere else. An end to fear is an end to *control* - especially religious control. It is an end to all ideas of right and wrong. It is an end to all ideas about self, or of beliefs about God, of opinions about prophets or gurus, or masters or avatars, about heaven or hell, concepts of the Plan or the so-called New Age - about anything. It is not an end to your mind, only to your own personal fixations and interpretations about any single thing whatever. Your mind will still exist to do your bidding, except now it will be at the bidding of your spirit, in cool clear and honest detachment. An end to fear.

Be more spontaneous. Trust your feelings and become a "momentary" person. Be gentle to yourself.

45. THE DANCING BUDDHA.   (Joy).

A Buddha is dancing. He holds a staff in his right hand. His left hand blesses the world.

This card tells us of yet another attribute of a self-realised human being. It is the defining one. JOY! Joy is a *feeling*. It acknowledges that spirit is the eternal reality. Humans often feel so guilty about feeling happy, especially the kind of happiness that takes them beyond self-consciousness. There is this ingrained suspicion that happiness comes, inevitably, at the expense, somewhere down the line, of a balancing bout of misery. Or, that joy is suspect: all right for children or lovers or mad people but not a useful thing for normal people - not practical for everyday life. Oh, pity the human race! What an error!

This dancing Buddha is holding a (black) staff in his right hand, indicating that his power comes in a vertical line directly from spirit. He dances, secure in his power, yet his eyes are turned compassionately to the ground and his left hand is outstretched in a blessing. This is a man who has found his source, has integrated his spirit with his personality, and, for his time remaining on earth, gives of his energy to the world. He is at home in a joyful, giving, universe. *Giving is no longer an obligation.* Love is unconditional. It expects nothing back. It comes out of the abundance of joy; for, like love, *joy is all there is!* He has gone beyond fear into joy. He has gone beyond self-consciousness into originality. He has gone beyond the vacillating mood swings of ego, generated by cause and effect. A total shift in consciousness. Joy is so far beyond happiness that we might call it "cosmic mind". It is not the transient astral feeling of ego gratification. Not mere happiness. Joy is the essence of eternal BEING. It is the inner knowing that we are an expansive part of something infinite, eternal and all loving. JOY *IS*.

The understanding that joy is a vibrational frequency of spirit will be the keynote of the age to come. So, maybe this is the most important card in this pack. From the recognition that joy and spirit are identical will come a loosening of the bonds of guilt - and a replacing of these bonds by a harmonic resonance which will arise in the planet, within humans and the environment alike, supporting all that lies within the aura of this living earth in a spirit of compassion, cooperation, and oft-time spontaneous celebration.

Understand, joy is the key to the future, both yours and the planet's. Once you know the truth of this, when you know it in your heart, there is no going back. Whether you like it or not, you are committed to bringing this frequency into reality by your own unique means of *BEING IT.* It is for you to find out what this means for you. It is for you, practically, to organise your life so that this is easy for you to do. It is for you *to hold this new (joy) frequency within yourself in your everyday life until finally it becomes crystallised into being your true and only reality.* THIS IS SELF REALISATION! This is life as a dance! A celebration! This is the only goal you have to achieve. Such a simple thing. Nothing to do. Nothing to struggle with. Just a letting go of all "doing", of all ideas, of all beliefs, of all plans, of all non-nourishing entanglements. You are to become a momentary person, living within your "moment". You are to live in a new space. It is a space of intuitive awareness rather than a mind-set of reason and logic. Mind is but lightly there as a creative servant but is no longer the master. Finally, please do remember that *joy does not arise out of any desire to be spiritual, but from an awareness of who you are.*

Take time out to feel how it would be if you were truly free. But you are!

46. A MAN WITH A WOODEN FISH. (Emotion).

A man dressed in pale flowing robes and a blue belt is cradling a carving of a wooden fish in his left arm. He is carrying a fly whisk over his left shoulder.

This person is at home with his feelings. His pale green robes flow around him like water. His solar plexus (emotional centre) is covered by a blue sash, indicating that he has his astral body well under control. The colour blue shows that spiritual vision (higher feelings), rather than feelings originating from desire, are the keynote of this personality. The fish he carries on his left side (the feminine receptive side) indicates his willingness to be yielding, sensitive and intuitive. There is nothing more sensitive or receptive to current than a fish in its watery element. This person is receptive to every nuance of his spirit by means of a highly developed - perhaps even psychic - intuition. Note well his fly whisk. This is to whisk away those unwanted, unruly, thoughts. Note also his expression of serenity, his general air of calm purpose. He honours his feelings, knowing that they are a part of him. Yet, he also knows his feelings are not *who he is.*

Emotion (feelings) are constantly at play within you irrespective of whether you are sitting or being active, being calm or being angry, being sexual or being celibate, being mentally focused or asleep. Your astral body loves to move. Like water, it is easily stirred into motion by any little breeze. Indeed, the word "emote" comes from the Latin, meaning to "put into motion". And what is this breeze which stirs your feelings? It is, of course, your mind. Now, if you become conscious of your feelings you can become conscious of what your mind is thinking. And, vice versa: if you can become conscious of what you are thinking, you will naturally be in control of how you feel. If you are not fully conscious of either your thoughts or your feelings, you have problems because your unconscious thoughts (your beliefs or attitudes) will make you have feelings you feel ashamed of - or feelings that catch you unawares which arise at inappropriate times. Further, if you deny unpleasant feelings, pretending that all is wonderful in your life, you are compounding the problem dramatically. In fact, you are building around your self the strong walls of a thoroughly conditioned ego. Indeed, this is all that the conditioned ego really is. Understanding this and ending denial of feelings is the challenge before humans in the next 2,000 years. To go through this door is to end separation and discover joy. There are no ifs and buts about this: each person has to do it for himself or herself, each in their own way. It cannot be legislated for by good government. It cannot be manifested by affirmations. Religion, mass prayer, or blind devotion, cannot make it happen. Only the individual, being awake, looking within, and making a search *of their own feelings and mental attitudes and beliefs* can make it happen.

Another factor to consider is that when you are in denial of feelings, you are unprotected from the emotional content of others. This is not a happy state of affairs. It produces a cyclic trigger effect (karma) which goes round and round until someone (hopefully it will be you!) does something about it.

Now, the wonderful thing about all this is that today, as never before on earth, there are many helpers ready to help you. When looking for a helper, trust your intuition, discover who is around, feel who is right for you. Don't become stuck with any one helper. Harness your will to do your own inner "work", and have courage! Most importantly, you will need to make yourself open and vulnerable - difficult for many - when exploring these wondrous feeling aspects of yourself. This is the greatest work you will ever do on this planet. See to it!

Awareness of your feelings and ending the denial of your feelings is an issue here.

47. THE WARRIOR.   (Discernment).

A warrior in golden armour is sitting astride a blue black-scaled dragon. It has small wings of fire coming out of its body. The warrior is carrying two staves in his right hand. He has a blue circular symbol over his heart and a jewel over his third eye. His helmet is emblazoned with jewels.

This is not a warrior charging into battle. This dragon is merely alert; happy to be sitting and to be at the bidding of his master (the golden spiritual self). In fact, this person is ready to fly on wings of spirit (the fire). There is a joyous strength here, accompanying new energy. There is also a new clarity here (see the jewel in the third eye).

The lure of knowledge, for its own sake, and the subtle control it once exerted over this personality, is over. Material knowledge has been transmuted by the alchemical process of the spiritual warrior into the spiritual vision of the cosmic self, the blue heart being the symbol of this. The gap has been crossed. Now a space has opened in which the soul can flower. It does so, magnificently, as its abundant golden self. In this space, which is neither of spirit nor of matter, there is a meeting of both - and yet it is also something entirely new. It is a new state of being beyond duality but which still lives in duality. It is a mode of consciousness that is hard to write about because it is of a higher consciousness than mind consciousness. In fact, trying to understand it with the mind will put you right back into duality. All I can say is, *it is a jump.* You reach a point in your life where, after much spiritual battling, the jump is so easy it can come upon you almost unawares. And yet, there is no danger that you might miss it. When the Self arrives and makes Self known to you, you cannot help but be immediately aware, how unaware - like to a state of sleep - was your previous awareness. So, how do you get to this point? By constant awareness and vigilance, by unwavering trust, by determination, by courage, by harnessing your will (and placing it along side the will of your higher self), by constant inner searching, by ending the denial of feelings, by meditation and contemplation, by never giving up (until you give up!) and lastly, but not least, by *discernment.*

The arena for the battles of the spiritual warrior is the self. This is indicated here by the symbols of duality (the two staves). Our warrior is holding them in his right hand, his sword hand, the hand of action. The earth plane is the plane of demonstration where love and joy need to be *actively* demonstrated, where duality needs to be *actively (not theoretically)* confronted and transcended. The spiritual warrior needs to accept the principles of duality whilst keeping free of its illusions. He or she cultivates discernment and approaches form from a perspective of his or her inner truth. There is no greater loss than to lose your awareness of your at-one-ment with the universe. Discernment is the means by which you avoid this. If you so fear loss that you cannot make choices, then you are lost. Detachment is the means by which you maintain a correct perspective of yourself as a spiritual entity living in apparent duality.

Your mind is your instrument of discrimination (by which you make choices). This is it's glory. This is for what it was designed. It has a sword-like quality that enables you to cut away old beliefs, discard outlived attitudes and keep at bay unwanted thoughts. You can use it like a searchlight to delve deep into the very foundations of your life, and become enlightened mind. It will help you to get to that final place from where you can jump beyond the mind or - better put - where the jump *happens to you.* Now the Self is realised.

Single-mindedness is required here. Do not wallow in excuses.

48. THE RED DEMON.   (Rage).

An angry red demon, surrounded by flames, is holding a club in both hands ready to smash at whoever, or whatever, enrages him.

Rage is a familiar emotion to all humans living on this planet. We have all seen or felt it at one time or another. It rises from within us like an all consuming fire. The rational mind goes out of the window. There is only the blind urge to destroy without care or compassion, without awareness or discrimination. There are degrees of anger; but rage is total. It is blind to anything other than the energy of its self. This card indicates such a state. It need not be altogether negative. There is energy available here for transformation.

Indeed, in a person of developed intuition, where goodwill is fundamentally present, the eruption of timely rage can mark the point of realisation that a situation in which feelings have been long denied is no longer to be tolerated. A new way of living, accompanied by a new attitude to one's life, takes the place of the old way. The old beliefs, previous patterns of behaviour, former ways of relating, are let go of. This is transformation. In most cases, this is essential psychological "work" that at some time in your life it will be necessary for you to explore. It sometimes goes under the name of primal therapy, re-birthing, or group work. Please understand, this is not therapy for people who have failed to make it in the world, it is for people who have made it but now wish to go beyond. It is for those brave souls who are the future of humanity. It is for those who wish to rediscover their roots - their true roots being none other than their own spirit.

An excellent way to explore long held denied feelings is in groups of people of similar "goodwill". This avoids the "throwing of your anger" on to another person (or blaming) which inevitably happens in one to one relationships. It must be said, however, that if fundamental goodwill (the will to change) is not present, no amount of rage or anger will be of use as a transforming energy. Anger without any willingness to make inner changes takes you off the boil - for the moment, yet the underlying cause (the inner heat) will remain - to rear its angry head, club in hand, another day.

Anger is a symptom of deep unease in your life. However, the reverse holds true. When life is easy there is no anger. Now, of course, life can only be easy and effortless when you trust in spirit. Incorrect identification with your role *rather than with your spirit* is the difficulty here. You cannot buy love, or joy, or peace, for services rendered. They do NOT depend on achievement, recognition, money, possessions, sex, a loving wife or family, or any other outer consideration. They are not a result of anything you will ever do (or ever have done) because *they are already an indelible part of who you already are.* Find out who you are (in other words, *become aware*) and anger will fall away.

Rage is a clash between your logical reasoning mind and your intuition (your link with spirit). Your mind locks out spirit's messages to you whilst capturing your emotional energy to provide it with the stimulus and nourishment to maintain, or rebuild, its pet construct; namely, your old friend the conditioned ego. The conflict between the two warring sides of yourself builds up potential until it generates a lightening flash (rage). Rage is a mental vomit, with an emotional spewing forth. It comes from incorrect mental alignment with your spirit. It comes from a lack of trust in the *Tao* (see Card 1.) and, above all, from ignorance as to your true nature. Rage can only exist where union is not realised.

Energy for transformation is available. Look deeper, and change your life.

49. THE ARCHITECT.   (Creativity).

A warrior is dressed in a luxurious red velvet robe over golden armour. All is trimmed in green. He is holding a model of a seven story building in his right hand. His left hand rests upon the hilt of his sword.

Here we have a beautiful card symbolic of one who is a master of creativity at every level (the seven tiered building) in this planetary system.   In one life-time or another this person has achieved self-realisation. It so happens that the physical plane, being the plane of *active demonstration,* is the most difficult level at which to demonstrate love. But, having done so, we become a master of creativity at all levels. The greatest creativity - generally misunderstood - is none other than the opening of oneself and others to ever more love. This you can do at any level. At the physical level it is a challenge which needs a deeply committed will.

The colour representing Cosmic Will (the will *to be)* is a beautiful ruby red. Crystal clear, powerful and magnificent. It is cool and clear - very different to the fiery murky reds seen in the aura as a result of the emotional passion of anger or lust. The mighty ruby ray of cosmic will is often shown alongside the golden ray, gold being the colour of well being - or *whole being.* You can be sure that the combination of these qualities, the ruby and the gold, within this entity, guarantees that, in whatever world this person sets foot, he or she will powerfully express *the joy of being.* See how strongly this figure stands upon the ground. See how his third eye, his spiritual vision, is open. See how all is lightly trimmed with the colour apple-green. This is the colour of harmony. Even his sword is green. His left hand, his intuition, is in tune with his spirit. It rests lightly upon his sword (his mind) - mind being the instrument of creation in the world of duality. His mind is his to command with wisdom.

Cosmic Will - the will *to be* - is an unfamiliar energy on earth. The will *to love* and the will *to heal* is more understood. The ruby ray is often called the destroyer ray, yet it is better called the ray of initiation. Those entities who are at home with its potency, who carry its vibration within them, are aware that BEING - irrespective of whatever they have DONE in the past or will ever DO in the future - is a state of divine realisation (BEINGNESS), that is, in itself the very essence of *the Tao* (the way of life, see Card 1).

Entities that carry this energy are not overly concerned with the day to day anxieties and problems that beset the average person on earth. Indeed, though they are aware of them, these weighty matters are not of their reality. Cosmic Will energy is an energy that is confronting to all who are dependent on results or achievement for feeling good about themselves. Thus it is highly creative in a higher sense for it confronts and thereby "destroys" all that is extraneous to truth. It is timely to reiterate that no amount of artistic masterpieces or great healing work or "planetary saving" will allow you to experience the magnificent ruby ray of Cosmic Will. Only the letting go of all acts, *and attachment to them*, opens the door to this great initiation. An entity carrying this energy may be recognised by a total disregard for their own personal life, an uncompromising commitment to their spirit, a childlike simplicity, an inviolate depth of inner strength and peace - and an outrageous sense of humour. Few there are that have achieved this level of realisation whilst upon the earth. Maybe you will be one of them - or, at the very least, maybe you have contacted this energy before and are now ready to contact it again.

Look again at what you are creating around you. Is it what you really want? Become as a child and enter your kingdom. Just BE.

50. CARRYING FIRE.   (Mind).

A man in green is carrying a basket of fire on his left arm. He has a sword at his back. His right hand is holding a fly whisk over his left shoulder.

Here we have a man - it could equally well be a woman - who has achieved a measure of harmony (the green) in his life, and, further more, has achieved the realisation that he is NOT essentially his mind (the basket of fire), but that his mind is a useful tool with which he can be creative in the world of form. Thus, a necessary perspective is maintained between his mind and *who he is.*

In the physical world of form the right side is our symbol for the active *outer* principle of mind (note the fly whisk in his right hand). It indicates he has learnt to whisk away those pesky thoughts which might disturb the clarity of his vision by contaminating it with emotion. The left side of mind is the receptive side, the vehicle for intuition, the active *inner* principle, that which can listen to the still small voice of spirit. The challenge here is not to become too receptive to the voice of the conditioned ego.

Mind is a highly creative principle, responsible for all that has been, or ever will be, created at *all levels in the universe.* All is mind, just as all is love and all is joy. You can no more rid yourself of your mind than cut off your head and still expect to survive on the physical plane. However, mind is of a substance that is more gross than spirit. Spirit has a prior origin than mind and is, therefore, closer to the source. The mind has the beautiful and unique characteristic of being able to discriminate and therefore to choose what - on your behalf - it wants to create. If, however, it makes for itself a *separate* identity - separate, that is, from spirit, it may create any manner of wonderful scenarios, but none of them will be in harmony with spirit. This is illusory ego. Conditioned ego. This will cause you anguish and, eventually, disease. Now, when you use your intuition to listen to spirit, you align your mind with spirit.

Integration results and harmony reigns. Peace is yours. An aura of grace, strength, love and joy, surrounds you. You are an inspiration to all on earth - especially to those who are still fascinated by, and caught up in, the web of their own mind; their own fearful ego being like a spider at the centre of it.

The mind operates so competently within the spheres of duality, that it may be difficult to believe there can be anything that is worthwhile beyond mind. Yet, there most definitely is. Trust and faith are helpful here. Development of the intuition is essential. A spirit fused personality is one in which the intuition takes precedence over mind. There is no other way by which to access your multi-dimensional cosmic self or to live on a day to day basis in tune with your spirit, than by trusting it. Your intuition is the magic key for doing this.

Duality is the mind's playing field. Stop being roped in to its games. Become, instead, the watcher. This is not ridding your self of mind, merely a placing of mind in perspective. It is, for the moment, putting it on one side so that *who you are* can reveal Itself to you as your true Self. When both the good and the bad in your life is seen and accepted as being "of the mind", you are ready for change. Visions of heaven and hell are duality fantasies. They are mind inspired. Like sex, they are dreams to follow - but to where, you might well ask? As a living reality they are not comparable to the reality of BEING in tune with spirit's peace. Finally, please remember, the ego mind abhors stillness. It loves to be busy. It will do anything to avoid being still. It is a past master at this. But, stillness is exactly what you need. You will come to love it.

To experience the power of the fantasies generated by your mind, take time out to observe how your mind functions. Become the watcher.

51. THE WOMAN AND THE FOX. (Sex).

A beautiful woman, richly adorned, leans to her right. She is glancing beguilingly out of the corner of her eyes. On her right side is a fox with a blue tail and blue mouth. In her left arm she is cradling a green and red broom. A pale blue amulet lies at her throat. A double-ended tassel hangs discreetly under her clothes.

This card holds all the mysteries and symbols of that marvellous activity which we call sex. Sex is an activity that all humans indulge in. It is a perfectly natural part of being human. The secret of the ages, long suppressed by religions more interested in control than in love and joy, is that, when linked to a higher emotional frequency, the energy generated through orgasm opens up higher centres (the chakras). Thus higher levels of vibrational frequency can be experienced. It can be used - especially in the case of women - to fly, via the mind, to other places and other levels in the universe.

This is what lay behind the medieval belief that witches fly on broomsticks - the stick being a symbol for the penis. In men, orgasm resulting from *aware sex* brings about a profound grounding of their divinity. The male feels complete and whole upon the physical plane. He feels at peace upon the earth. His goddess, meanwhile - his "ear unto god" - may fly, via her mind, to other realms to enhance her knowledge and wisdom, to renew her faith and purpose, and to bring back to her partner that part of the creative plan seen from a wider perspective; which is now theirs to implement together. Thus do the *yin* and the *yang* work together in the implementing of the grand creative plan for earth, being the creation of an environment in which more love and joy can be experienced. Indeed, this planet will one day be known as the planet of "the dancing sparks".

When sex is relaxed, *joyful and total,* and there is a natural overflowing of sexual energies, then this can happen. First, you must believe it can happen. Second, you must create a space for it to happen. After orgasm, become intensely still. Go into meditation - *and become aware.*

Sex, without love or joy present, indulged in purely for relief (as in compulsive masturbation),or as a means of control, or out of a sense of duty or habit, or for the fulfilment of some desire - even the desire to make a baby, does not open these higher centres. Joyless sex can become a chronic addiction, strengthening the denial of feelings, concretising the ego and increasing your separation from spirit. It must, inevitably, lead to disease in the personality. The reason for this is that you are not merely of human form. A part of your nature lies beyond the physical form. Aware sex not only puts you in touch with this part, but also integrates your non-physical Self with your human self, which, indeed, is the goal for all on earth. Unaware sex keeps you form bound, unleavened by your spiritual nature.

In aware sex, energy from your sex centre activates your throat centre (note the blue energy in both the tail and the mouth of the fox!). From your throat centre you sound out your vibrational frequency upon the earth, creating your human self in your divine image. This happens naturally when your sexual activities are without guilt or shame, and when - and only when - sex is a loving joyful act of true union for both parties! The orgasm will move energy through your higher centres. Masturbation is of little harm when the whole body is involved, and when the mind remains clear of fantasies. But, addiction to release is very harmful. When you fantasise, your mind-energy goes out from you to create harmful thought-forms in the astral realms. These will drain you of energy and are harmful to others. Rise above sexual addictions.

Examine your sex life. Be aware of all the energies involved.

52. CARRYING THE FLAG. (Loyalty).

A young man triumphantly holds aloft a flag upon which is a cross of bones within a circle of bones. His right hand is thrust forward; his left hand is thrust behind his back to his right side. He is wearing a pink suit, white head band, blue belt and red boots.

We all know of someone who is proud to be carrying a flag for someone - perhaps for their school or their teacher, perhaps for their political party or their regiment or their country, perhaps for their religion or their master. However, whoever and whatever we carry a flag for, *unless we are - first and foremost listening to - and trusting, our own spirit*, it will all turn out to be dry, dry bones!

To the Chinese a cross is a symbol of misfortune. It means the way is blocked, energy is misdirected or the *Tao is* misunderstood. Yet, here we have a young man who is enthusiastically proclaiming that his way is the right way. He is shouting it out to the world, thoroughly convinced that his cause is the *right* cause to follow. But note that his *left* hand, his intuitive, receptive, side, is behind his back. Indeed, it maybe the right cause for *him* to believe in if he is following his spirit. Unfortunately, it becomes confused when he is influencing others to his path when they should be following theirs.

Young souls are vulnerable souls. They are easily led by dreams of glory to follow a flag which in the long run only leads them into confusion. A spirit-fused personality follows no flag but that which softly flutters in the light breeze of their own intuitive heart. Their *own* heart! A spirit-fused personality has no loyalty but to their own god within. A spirit-fused personality surrenders to no master but the master within their own heart. Any outer surrender or outer loyalty, is merely temporary - *for the meantime*. There is an old Zen saying: "If you meet the Buddha on the path, kill him!" This is metaphorical, of course. It might be better to say: "Whenever you hear of a spiritual master, approach with caution!" You need to trust your feelings, your common sense and your intuition (your link to your spirit) at all times. Experience what the "master" has to offer, *then move on!* Don't get caught up in any situation that doesn't have a clarity in it from your personal perspective. Many are the woes that foolish disciples bring upon themselves and others through misplaced idealism and blind fanaticism.

A self-realised person - and, is this not your goal - has the self-confidence to stand alone. Your first loyalty is to your own self; only then to others, respecting and treating others as you would yourself. You are to become a self-empowered, self-motivated, entity; being dependent on nothing outside of yourself, no person, no master, no group, no special family, no angels, no twin soul, and no cosmic beings. Yes, of course, you may love all these. They do exist! Of course, you can experience a joy in being a part of it all. Indeed, if you don't accept it all now, you will one day have to, *but you will never be dependent on, or beholden to, any of it.*

Only when you can stand alone will you discover your place within the whole and the unique role that is yours - and only yours - to play. You are rather special. You have a niche. You - and no one else - was created for that niche. That alone makes you special. BUT, please, have no opinions about it. Go beyond self-consciousness, go beyond following the herd and go beyond following anyone else's flag - however dazzling it might appear.

A situation has arisen where you need to take stock: whose tune are you dancing to? Can you say truthfully that it is your very own?

53. THE WATCHER.   (Meditation).

A man is sitting in meditation on a mat. His left hand, under his robe, is raised toward his head. The flag above him states that this is "the flag of a hundred souls."

This man is calling souls to himself. He is one who patiently watches and waits. When a soul is ready for what he has to offer, he makes himself known: thus, demonstrating the truth of the old saying: *"When the pupil is ready the master appears."*

This card could equally apply to you who are *calling out* to your own soul (your own multi-dimensional self) which is, after all, your own personal master. When you sit in meditation, you are in communion with that which is beyond your daily preoccupations and limited perception. Through meditation you are inviting your fully realised self to make itself known to you. Indeed, meditation (and contemplation) needs to becomes an essential part of a seeker's life. Nothing is attained without it. It is the way. It is the *Tao*. And after liberation it is still the way.

Before your whole self can merge with your personality self, your personality (the ego mind) must first empty itself of all opinions and all ideas of itself. A spirit-fused personality is one that trusts in spirit uncompromisingly - yes, even to the point of the "death" of the personality. Note, death is not actively sought after. This would be a subtle, controlling, demand, and a violence to the self. What is required is a total longing for liberation - *and nothing else.* "Ask and ye shall receive." Such a commitment needs to go alongside courage, acceptance, patience and, above all, an habitual watchfulness. Without watchfulness your mind will be too full of its own opinions and ideas - be they the most sublime of spiritual aspirations. Experiencing the ALL-THAT-IS is a *feeling* experience within the physical body. To become full you must become empty of all ideas - and all desire. Joy is to be found in the spaces of life - between this and that!

Meditation, as in contemplation, is the key which creates the environment in which enlightenment can happen. Meditation as the magic formula, however, or as an exercise to "get you there", is counter productive. Meditation that mesmerises you into being less than fully "alive" in the world, that removes you from your physical plane reality, or alienates you from your personality, is not useful. It can lead to delusions of spiritual arrogance and a hopelessly unbalanced personality. Remember, you are here to be liberated in your body here on earth, while your physical body and personality are in attendance. The physical plane is a part of the whole. You cannot become whole without it! Do not go off into beautiful day dreams about going into nirvana to be whole or free. Dreams they will remain!

Contemplation (becoming the watcher) is required; but it is useless if it just leads to fantasies. As in everything, discrimination - and an awareness of the here-and-now - and being grounded upon the physical plane *within your physical body*, is essential. A good rule for spiritual practice is: if it dissolves neurosis (anxiety) it is good for you. If it creates or maintains anxiety, let it go. Maybe it is time for you to surrender, to relax, or time to move on to something else. Contemplation is the final step. It is just to sit and BE. It is to look without looking. It is to allow existence to fall into you.

Lie or sit, preferably in nature. Find the silence between your thoughts and remain for a while in that silence. Look into the space between your thoughts. What is this space? Who is there?

54. THE WINGED DEMON.
(Death).

A green winged demon is flying through the air holding on to a staff. He is wearing garments of white, black and red.

Death! There is no such thing! So, the very word should be abolished. When the word *death* is no longer used, the belief in its permanency - as being the end of all conscious personality - will end. The gateway to a greater life, indeed, an ever extending vista of conscious life will be seen to lie ahead for humans.

For the unenlightened masses death takes on the aspect of a fearsome spectre as depicted in this card. It comes - often suddenly or when least expected - on swift wings. Its power (note the rod of power held in both hands of this demon) is not to be denied. All of us will be meeting death sooner or later. Are we ready for this adventure - the very last of physical plane moments we are destined to experience in this life-time? The answer, is probably *Yes* if we know it to be but a change-over from one reality to another. But probably *No* if we view death as the end of everything. Ignorance is a fertile breeding ground for fear, is it not?

Apart from actually relinquishing the physical body for a body composed of a finer substance, *death* can also be a form of a psychological change from one reality to another. It may result in the letting go of long held beliefs (or attitudes) together with the release of emotional energy locked in with them. Whilst alive on earth, we may go through many similar mini-deaths as part of the rites of passage (initiations) that we go through during our search for self-realisation. This is the meaning of the phrase "to be born again." In fact, every night when we go to sleep we "die" do we not, to be miraculously born again in the morning. The process of final physical death is much like it.

The belief that death is the final extinguishment of the personality is a belief of absolutely incredible ignorance. This belief alone holds within it much of the world's fear and despair, its cynicism and possessiveness, its competitiveness, its cruelty, its judgement and vengeance. Are these not dreadful words to be using about such a lovely blue-green planet? They are all found to be bound up with that emotionally loaded word *death*. A better word by far - as most of you well know - is *change*.

An aware entity takes responsibility for all change. At some level of your being you are always responsible for what is happening to yourself. The process called *death* contains within it both the greatest of lessons, and great joy. The aware entity watches the process of change with interest, with curiosity, and with loving support, and appreciation, knowing that change is as natural to it as breathing. Change IS the very nature of life. It is the ebb and flow of life. An enlightened entity lives in the peace of a quiet soft space, the non-changing, observing the ever changing. To find this magical space is the quest you are embarked upon: giving up so much for it may well seem, at times, like dying. Fear exists when there is resistance to change. Acceptance of change (and acceptance of the fear also, if any there be) is the key to a joyful and easy transition from one octave of consciousness to another. But, remember, you are here for a reason: *spiritual growth can only be attained on the physical plane.* After you leave, it is re-assessment time. Don't miss the opportunity!

The gift of personality is this loving universe's gift to you. Your personality doesn't die. Be assured of this. Your conditioned ego is another matter. Remember: cosmic self plus personality is who you are. Cosmic self plus personality *plus conditioned ego* is you carrying excess baggage!

Don't take yourself so seriously. Death is always around the corner. Greet it as an old friend. It's message is to end control, to relax, to laugh, to enjoy - and to allow others to do the same.

55. THE DRAGON OF WISDOM.
(Liberation).

A fiery dragon is holding two blue discs in its claws. It has a scarf of gold tied around its chest.

In western medieval symbolism the dragon was often seen as evil or as being a symbol for our earth nature - our personal instincts - which needed to be tamed or subdued. In ancient Egypt, however, the dragon was associated with the solar god Thoth, the god of wisdom and the star Sirius (the dog star or *dragon star*). Then again, a Druid of the ancient Celts would say: "I am a Druid. I am a Dragon."

Unlike Westerners, The Chinese have always regarded the dragon with reverence and respect. To the Chinese, the dragon is a creature of awesome power and mystical knowledge. The dragon can equally bring good or bad fortune. The dragon is seen as guarding a secret treasure. Most Chinese festivals involve homage to the dragon.

In fact, in ancient Asia the term *dragon* was the accepted term for a person who had achieved liberation. These great souls were known as The Dragons of Wisdom. The dragon - the fiery serpent - represented wisdom, immortality and rebirth. For, as the serpent sheds its skin of scales so does the immortal Self cast off one personality at will and assume another. When a human personality becomes fused consciously with spirit, a Dragon of Wisdom (a master) is said to walk the land. In due time, this master, earth-service completed, would retire under a cloak of invisibility (another of the dragon's magical attributes) to sit and watch the world from another place, holding it in love and compassion, perhaps teaching an inner circle of disciples.

The dragon is not shown in the form of a person because he or she has gone beyond the ego-conditioned personality. Something new has been born in which nothing of value has been lost. The word *dragon* comes from a word meaning *"The one who excels in intelligence"* or *"He who sees and watches"*. These masters of wisdom still live in duality but within themselves have reconciled the opposites. Traditionally, the dragon guards a treasure. The doorway to this treasure is said to be through a portal of spinning discs (note the blue discs this dragon is clutching). An ancient Tibetan commentary says: *"The victor is projected from the dragon's fiery crest to that vibrating disc which guards the fourfold door of luminosity."*

Wisdom is a combination of love and knowledge. The mind is neither over potent nor under developed. There is neither control nor undue passivity. The critical faculties are in balance. Harmony reigns.

With this in mind, let us look more closely at some other dragon symbols. The fire on its tail, for instance, and the even greater fire on its head (the crest) shows us that the inner energies have been lifted upward without denying those rooted in the body. The gold cloth around the chest shows that the golden treasure is to be found by way of the heart. Dragons traditionally breathe fire. Only by the *burning away* of all fears, illusions, limiting beliefs, elitist ambition, creative desires, identity roles and all other attachments, do we return, fully conscious, to the way of the heart and make the treasure our own. Then we see that at no time have we been without the treasure. Indeed, we see that the treasure never has been *guarded*. It was merely *hidden* - within us. Dragons are helpful. Do not be afraid of these dragons who have been watching you patiently with such love, for so long. It is the very last thing they would wish. For, remember, they too were once - not so long ago - where you are now.

Of the Masters of Compassion little can be said. Honour them.

AN INSTANT GUIDE

TO THE DRAGON-WISDOM CARDS OF ANCIENT CHINA.

Note, this quick guide is best used as an *aide memoire*. It is not to be taken as a truthful or accurate rendering of the DRAGON-WISDOM CARDS. Meditation upon the commentaries together with your own intuitive insight at the time a question is asked, or a reading given, is the recommended way to access the wisdom of the DRAGON-WISDOM CARDS. The guide emphasises the positive qualities to which each card points.

1. THE TAO (The Way)............................. The way is *your* way.

2. THE HEADLESS MAN ON
    THE TIGER (No direction)..................... Recreate your vision

3. THE MAN ON THE BUFFALO
    (Resignation)..................................... Re-ignite your
                                                      spiritual life.

4. THE GIRL AND THE PEACOCK
    (Beauty) .... Beauty with self-
                                                      realisation endures.

5. THE DEMON (Desire) .... Acknowledge
                                                  attachment to desires.

6. A MAN WITH A GOURD
    (Poisonous Thoughts)........................ Be aware of the power
                                                  of your thoughts.

To Purchase
The packs of cards (55 cards) of **THE DRAGON-WISDOM CARDS OF ANCIENT CHINA**
contact
markkumara@gmail.com

To Purchase
THE JOY OF BEING (285 pages of inspirational spiritual teaching) **by Mark Kumara**.
contact
www.trafford.com

To purchase further copies of this book **THE DRAGON-WISDOM CARDS OF ANCIENT CHINA and Commentaries on The Tao**
contact
www.trafford.com